Wakefield Press

THE NANCY SINGH LETTERS

THE NANCY SINGH LETTERS

NANCY SINGH

Wakefield Press

Wakefield Press
1 The Parade West
Kent Town
South Australia 5067
www.wakefieldpress.com.au

First published 2010

Designed by Dean Lahn, Lahn Stafford Design
Typeset by Clinton Ellicott, Wakefield Press
Printed and bound by Hyde Park Press, Adelaide

National Library of Australia Cataloguing-in-Publication entry

Author:	Singh, Nancy.
Title:	The Nancy Singh letters/Nancy Singh.
ISBN:	978 1 86254 848 0 (pbk.).
Subjects:	Singh, Nancy – Correspondence.
	Public officers – Correspondence.
	Australia – Officials and employees – Correspondence.
Dewey Number:	A826.4

For Mr. Singh and Mr. Joe Hockey,
the men I love

July 1, 2008

Mr. Peter Garrett MP
Minister for the Environment

NANCY SINGH (MRS)
PO Box 5067
South Murwillimbah
New South Wales 2484
Import and Export Services

Dear Mr. Garrett

Now that you have some time on your hands and Penny Wong (isn't she amazing!) is doing the water portfolio, I am writing to ask if you would consider re-forming your pop group *Midnight Oil* for a last tour? I have had an idea that you could raise money for the poor people of Burma and China, or even the orangutans. Even small gestures can have an impact.

I hope you will not mind my asking for a signed photograph of you. I know that every penny matters, so here is $5 for the postage. Keep up the good work.

Sincerely,

Mrs. Nancy Singh

July 1, 2008

Miss Julie Bishop MP

NANCY SINGH (MRS)
PO Box 5067
South Murwillimbah
New South Wales 2484
Import and Export Services

Dear Miss Bishop,

I am writing to say how wonderful it was to see you humble Mr. Wayne Swan in Parliament over his so-called advice on saving money when food shopping. Mr. Swan clearly knows as much about household economics as Mark Latham knew about manners and breeding.

Mr. Singh tells me that you are easily the most attractive lady MP in the House. I was wondering if you would send him a signed photograph of your good self, as it is his birthday later this month. I am enclosing $5 to cover the postage.

Many thanks,

Sincerely,

Mrs. Nancy Singh

Julie Bishop

Federal Member for Curtin
Deputy Leader of the Opposition
Shadow Minister for Employment, Business and Workplace Relations

Nancy Singh
PO Box 5067
South Murwillimbah NSW 2484
Postal Address

29 July 2008

Dear Nancy

Thankyou for your letter to the Hon Julie Bishop, I have enclosed a picture as requested.

Please also find enclosed your $5.00 as it is not necessary for you to pay for the postage.

Please pass on Ms Bishop's birthday wishes to Mr Singh.

Best wishes

KRidge

KIRSTEN RIDGE

Curtin Includes:
Churchlands
City Beach
Claremont
Cottesloe
Crawley
Daglish
Dalkeith
Doubleview*
Floreat
Glendalough
Jolimont
Joondanna
Karrakatta
Leederville
Mosman Park
Mt. Claremont
Mt. Hawthorn
Nedlands
North Perth*
Osborne Park*
Peppermint Grove
Shenton Park
Subiaco
Swanbourne
Wembley
Wembley Downs
West Leederville
West Perth*
Woodlands

*Part Suburbs

Julie Bishop

414 Rokeby Road, SUBI 4)
Tel: (08) 9388 0288 Fax: (08) 9388 0299 juli bishop.com.au

July 1, 2008

NANCY SINGH (MRS)
PO Box 5067
South Murwillimbah
New South Wales 2484
Import and Export Services

Mr. Kevin Rudd MP
Prime Minister

Dear Mr. Rudd,

Many congratulations to you on your first 6 months in office, and such a sensible budget. I am not one of those who argue that Wayne Swan is out of his depth, and I am sure he will stop stumbling over his words soon.

I think it is a great idea to forge closer links with China, and who could be better placed to do this than your good self. I myself am in the import-export business and am always on the lookout for cheap goods to sell here in Australia.

I hope you will not mind my asking for a signed photograph of you. In these inflationary times I know that every penny matters, so here is $5 for the postage.

Sincerely,

Mrs. Nancy Singh

July 1, 2008

NANCY SINGH (MRS)
PO Box 5067
South Murwillimbah
New South Wales 2484
Import and Export Services

Mr. Glenn Stevens,
Governor of the Federal Reserve Bank

Dear Mr. Stevens,

I am writing to ask your advice on a financial matter. In these inflationary times is it better to invest in government bonds or shares in the energy sector? I suppose this depends on how long it will take your policy of increasing interest rates to bring down the price of petrol?

I am quite happy with the rates being high as I do not have a mortgage, am earning interest on my savings accounts, and there are so many bargains to be had in clothes and plasma televisions. But the petrol prices are annoying and I have taken to driving my Audi rather than the Mercedes. On the plus side, it is easier to drive around and find a park, now that the poor are being priced off the road. A good dose of redundancies would be an added benefit, and it is reassuring that this is the bank's policy for the next few years.

Sincerely,

Mrs. Nancy Singh

July 8, 2008

NANCY SINGH (MRS)
PO Box 5067
South Murwillimbah
New South Wales 2484
Import and Export Services

The Chancellor
Griffith University

Dear Sir,

I read with great interest that your university is receiving funding from Saudi Arabia to establish new courses and award degrees. I am all in favour of market forces helping to pay for higher education.

One of my sons is not especially intelligent, but he has his heart set on being a Doctor. His father agrees that this would be better than allowing him to work in the family business. So we would like to buy him the necessary qualifications at your fine establishment. Please would you advise me on the best way to do this.

I am enclosing $5 to open our account in the meantime.

Sincerely,

Mrs. Nancy Singh

Office of the Pro-Vice Chancellor
(Administration)

Colin McAndrew
Pro-Vice Chancellor (Administration)

Nathan campus, Griffith University
170 Kessels Road
Nathan, Queensland 4111
Australia

Telephone +61 (0)7 3735 7343
Facsimile +61 (0)7 3735 7507

c.mcandrew@griffith.edu.au
www.griffith.edu.au

23 July 2008

Mrs Nancy Singh
PO Box 5067
SOUTH MURWILLIMBAH NSW 2484

Dear Mrs Singh

I refer to your letter to the Chancellor dated 8 July 2008. In this letter you make reference to the grant from the government of Saudi Arabia which was given to the University last year and which was the subject of newspaper articles in late April 2008.

The Saudi grant was donated to support the work of the Griffith Islamic Research Unit (GIRU). The central aim of GIRU is to promote a balanced and contextualised understanding of Islam and Muslims. GIRU, through its strong academic, community and government partnerships, provides a forum where scholars, intellectuals, and students can voice their insights, concerns, reflections and aspirations on issues facing the Australian Muslim community and the wider Australian community, with a view to cultivating an informed public opinion that will lead to a more sustainable pluralistic Australian society.

On the second issue raised in your letter, I would like to emphasise Griffith's commitment to rigorous standards of scholarship and to the pursuit of excellence in teaching and research. We repudiate any suggestion that degree qualifications can be bought from our University.

I return your original letter including the five dollar 'donation'.

Yours sincerely,

A C McAndrew
Pro Vice Chancellor
(Administration)

July 8, 2008

Director of Complaints
ABC

NANCY SINGH (MRS)
PO Box 5067
South Murwillimbah
New South Wales 2484
Import and Export Services

Dear Sir,

I am writing to complain at a quite disgraceful lapse of decency during a recent broadcast of 'Q and A'. I distinctly heard someone in the audience refer to one of the women panelists as a 'tart who doesn't wear knickers'. This is insulting to women, even those who occasionally go *al fresco*, often for perfectly good reasons.

I am appalled that you should allow this sort of thing to be broadcast to the nation.

Sincerely,

Mrs. Nancy Singh

14 July 2008

ABC
Australian
Broadcasting
Corporation

Mrs Nancy Singh
PO Box 5067
MURWILLUMBAH SOUTH NSW 2484

ABC Ultimo Centre
700 Harris Street
Ultimo NSW 2007

GPO Box 9994
Sydney NSW 2001

Tel. +61 2 8333 1500
abc.net.au

Dear Mrs Singh

Thank you for your letter of 8 July 2008.

The concerns outlined in your letter are currently being investigated. The ABC endeavours to respond to all letters within 28 days of receipt. However, please be aware that due to the large volume of correspondence we receive, and the complex nature of some enquiries, responses may at times take longer than four weeks.

I enclose a copy of our complaint handling fact sheet for reference.

Yours sincerely

Emma Callaghan
ABC Audience & Consumer Affairs

13 August 2008

ABC Ultimo Centre
700 Harris Street
Ultimo NSW 2007

GPO Box 9994
Sydney NSW 2001

Tel. +61 2 8333 1500
abc.net.au

Mrs Nancy Singh
PO Box 5067
MURWILLUMBAH SOUTH NSW 2484

Dear Mrs Singh

Thank you for your letter of 8 July 2008 regarding a comment you heard in a recent broadcast of Q & A.

We have reviewed the program of 3 July and did not hear a comment from an audience member that one of the women panellists was "a tart who doesn't wear knickers".

I would like to assure you that if an audience member had made that statement, the production team would not have wanted it to go to air and be audible to the viewer at home.

Thank you again for taking the time to write. I do hope this information allays your concerns.

For your reference, I have included a copy of the ABC's Code of Practice.

Yours sincerely

Claire M Gorman
Investigations Officer
ABC Audience & Consumer Affairs

July 8, 2008

NANCY SINGH (MRS)
PO Box 5067
South Murwillimbah
New South Wales 2484
Import and Export Services

Mrs. Justine Eliot MP
Minister for Ageing

Dear Mrs. Eliot,

Many congratulations on your elevation to the important post of Minister for Ageing. It is good to see our local MP moving so swiftly up the parliamentary pole.

Your portfolio is very important indeed. As a more mature lady myself, I am always on the lookout for new products and approaches to hold back the years and the wrinkles! I swear by a six-monthly botox and the use of Clarins night cream. Works a treat.

I hope you will not mind my offering you this tip. We ladies need to keep our little secrets from the men.

Sincerely,

Mrs. Nancy Singh

July 8, 2008

NANCY SINGH (MRS)
PO Box 5067
South Murwillimbah
New South Wales 2484
Import and Export Services

Miss Jenny Macklin MP
Minister for Families and Aborigines

Dear Miss Macklin,

I quite agree with your comments on old Mabo spinning in his grave. He would be horrified by the new depths his people have sunk to, caused by grog, welfare dependency and sexual deviance. The only answer, as you quite rightly say, is to get them off their backsides and working in the coalmines. A job, a wage and a good woman to keep them right is what these lazy men need.

I am glad we now have a strong woman responsible for Aboriginal affairs and look forward to a new dawn of decency and propriety.

Sincerely,

Mrs. Nancy Singh

July 8, 2008

Mrs. Belinda Neal MP

NANCY SINGH (MRS)
PO Box 5067
South Murwillimbah
New South Wales 2484
Import and Export Services

Dear Mrs. Neal,

I am writing to wish you well in your current disagreement with Joe Iguana and his staff. As a businesswoman myself, I know how difficult it is to get good staff. Honestly, they act like they own the place.

I myself am downsizing as employing people is too much hassle these days. I am pleased the government is doing its best to push up unemployment, as this will bring lazy so-called 'working families' to heel.

We need people like you in Parliament to tell it like it is.

Sincerely,

Mrs. Nancy Singh

July 8, 2008

Miss Tanya Plibersek
Minister for Housing

NANCY SINGH (MRS)
PO Box 5067
South Murwillimbah
New South Wales 2484
Import and Export Services

Dear Miss Plibersek,

I am writing to disassociate myself and Mr. Singh from comments in our local newspaper that you are not up to the onerous responsibility of running caravan parks for the so-called homeless. I have run caravan parks in my time and know how difficult this is, but I have every faith in your abilities.

Mr. Singh agrees with me, and he also says that you have the best legs of any minister on the front bench. He has asked if you would send a signed photograph of yourself (head and shoulders will do!). Please find enclosed $5 for postage.

Sincerely,

Mrs. Nancy Singh

July 8, 2008

Miss Nicola Roxon MP
Minister for Health

NANCY SINGH (MRS)
PO Box 5067
South Murwillimbah
New South Wales 2484
Import and Export Services

Dear Miss Roxon,

I am writing to castigate you in the strongest possible terms for increasing the cost of my favourite tipple, Bacardi Breezer, and those of fellow members of the Currumbin Ladies Magic Circle. We are not silly young girls who don't know how to say no. We have been saying no all our lives.

People of lower class around here are now simply buying bottles of vodka and cola and mixing their own. This is making matters worse.

I am wondering if you are related to Lillian Roxon, member of the Sydney Push, a self-selecting group of libertines and heavy drinkers. Now there was a group of people who could never say no!

Sincerely,

Mrs. Nancy Singh

July 12, 2008

NANCY SINGH (MRS)
PO Box 5067
South Murwillimbah
New South Wales 2484
Import and Export Services

Director of Complaints
SBS Television

Dear Sir,

I read an article recently about how SBS is having to compromise its principles to remain relevant in these shallow post-modern times. I certainly agree that there is little to watch on SBS for us ladies, not enough on plastic surgery or dieting for example, or tips on how to look good buying from op shops.

I think it is good that you have *Top Gear* for the boys. Mr. Singh loves it, although he does get a bit frisky on Monday nights after watching all of those skids and throbbing engines. At least they are not all homosexuals like everyone else on TV!

I think you should stick to your guns and keep SBS as it is, although you could get rid of all those foreign language films that nobody watches.

Sincerely,

Mrs. Nancy Singh

SBS Corporation - Australia's multicultural broadcaster

9448

23 July 2008

Mrs Nancy Singh
PO Box 5067
South Murwillimbah NSW 2484

Dear Mrs Singh,

Thank you for your letter.

We will pass on your comments to our Programming department for their consideration.

Yours sincerely

Erika Verolin
Public Relations

Locked Bag 028 Crows Nest NSW 1585 Australia
14 Herbert St, Artarmon NSW 2064 . Telephone (612) 9430 2828 . Facsimile (612) 9430 3700 . www.sbs.com.au

July 12, 2008

Mr. Harry Jenkins MP
Leader of the House

NANCY SINGH (MRS)
PO Box 5067
South Murwillimbah
New South Wales 2484
Import and Export Services

Dear Mr. Jenkins,

I am writing to ask your advice. I have been watching the Parliament on TV as I seek to understand how your democracy works. At times I find it confusing.

I am wondering:

Why it is called 'Question Time' if no questions are allowed to be asked?

Why no ministers ever answer a question that is asked?

Are you called Mr. Speaker Sir because you get to talk the most?

I wonder if you would also send me a signed photograph of your good self.

Sincerely,

Mrs. Nancy Singh

July 22, 2008

NANCY SINGH (MRS)
PO Box 5067
South Murwillimbah
New South Wales 2484
Import and Export Services

Mr. Anthony Albanese MP
Leader of the House

Anthony A...
Federal Member for Gray...
Received:
2 5 JUL 2008
Electorate Office

Dear Mr. Albanese,

I am writing to ask your advice. I am looking for a job with a very good pension, free travel and other perks, and attractive working hours and conditions. Like you, English is a second language for me, and I am not especially bright. I was wondering how I could get a job as Leader of the House? This seems not to involve a great deal of actual work.

I wonder if you would also send me a signed photograph of your good self. I am enclosing $5 to cover the postage.

Sincerely,

Mrs. Nancy Singh

July 22, 2008

NANCY SINGH (MRS)
PO Box 5067
South Murwillimbah
New South Wales 2484
Import and Export Services

Mr. John Brumby
Premier, Victoria

Dear Mr. Brumby,

I am writing to express my dismay that you are prepared to destroy the Murray-Darling for political advantage. A great many people dislike Mr. Rudd intensely, and he may be an imbecile, but this is not the way to get rid of him. Anyway, he is surely to be preferred to Red Julia?

I myself was recently in Albury, and could see no evidence of drought. It was freezing cold too, and I share your view, reported in *The Age* that 'global warning' is a 'complete load of tosh'.

Sincerely,

Mrs. Nancy Singh

Minister for Water

121 Exhibition Street
Melbourne, Victoria 3000
GPO Box 4509
Melbourne, Victoria 3001
Telephone: (03) 8684 8000
Facsimile: (03) 8684 8014

Ref: DSE055278
File: II/03/0070 - 4

Mrs Nancy Singh
PO Box 5067
MURWILLUMBAH SOUTH NSW 2484

29 SEP 2008

Dear Mrs Singh

MURRAY-DARLING BASIN

I refer to your letter dated 22 July 2008 to the Premier, the Hon. John Brumby MP, regarding the Murray-Darling Basin. As this issue falls within my responsibilities as the Minister for Water, your correspondence has been forwarded to me for a response.

The Victorian Government shares your concerns about the degradation of the Murray-Darling Basin, and is committed to restoring this important river system to good health as soon as possible.

As you may be aware, on 3 July 2008, the six Murray-Darling Basin Governments signed an Intergovernmental Agreement (IGA) to implement the historic Memorandum of Understanding agreed to at the Council of Australian Governments (COAG) in March 2008.

The IGA undertakes to meet current critical water needs across the Basin and provide a sustainable and secure future for farmers, communities and the environment. It includes establishing a new and independent organisation, the Murray-Darling Basin Authority. This Authority will set basin-wide caps on irrigation diversions and develop the Basin Plan to restore stressed rivers to good health and secure water supplies for human use.

The Commonwealth has also committed to provide up to $103 million for the Sunraysia Modernisation Project, to upgrade irrigation infrastructure around Merbein, Mildura and Red Cliffs. This is in addition to up to $1 billion committed in March to Stage 2 of the Northern Victoria Irrigation Renewal Project (NVIRP).

The Commonwealth funding commitments support the Victorian Government's continued focus on fixing leaky and inefficient irrigation systems to save water for the environment, rather than buying water on the market.

The rivers will be among the greatest beneficiaries of irrigation modernisation. For example, stages 1 and 2 of NVIRP will save 425 billion litres of real water now being lost through evaporation, seepage and system inefficiencies. The environment's 175 billion litre share of these savings is more than Adelaide consumes in a year, and will make a real difference to the health of the Murray River. Modernisation will ensure this water stays in rivers, where it belongs, rather than being wasted through evaporation and seeping into the ground where it raises water tables and contributes to salinity and soil waterlogging.

In the meantime, we all have to accept that current water availability is dependent on how much it has rained and the volumes in storage. The drought over the last 12 years has drained water storages down to extremely low levels – so low this year that Basin Governments have had to adopt special measures to make sure there is enough for critical human needs such as drinking water. Unless there is substantial rainfall in coming months, allocations will remain low for all users, including irrigators and the environment

You mention in your letter that Albury appears to be unaffected by drought. However, despite some rain during winter, storage levels still remain at record lows. This is because, after more than a decade of rainfall deficits and record high temperatures, it will take years of above-average rainfall to replenish the dams and return the rivers to health. In the meantime, winter rain has been enough to 'green' the paddocks, and hence create an illusion that the region is not drought affected.

Thank you for writing to the Government on these issues.

Yours sincerely

TIM HOLDING MP
Minister for Water

July 22, 2008

NANCY SINGH (MRS)
PO Box 5067
South Murwillimbah
New South Wales 2484
Import and Export Services

Mr. Maurice Iemma
Premier
New South Wales

Dear Mr. Iemma,

I am writing to say how sorry I am to hear that you are having trouble with your Labor cactus. I know how this feels. Although it seems cruel, I have found that the best way to deal with them is to lock them away in a hot room without drink. This tends to set the little pricks to rights.

I hope you will not mind my asking for a signed photograph of you. In these inflationary times I know that every penny matters, so here is $5 for the postage.

Sincerely,

Mrs. Nancy Singh

Nancy,
Best Wishes,

July 22, 2008

NANCY SINGH (MRS)
PO Box 5067
South Murwillimbah
New South Wales 2484
Import and Export Services

Miss Julia Lester
Classic FM
ABC

Dear Julia,

I am writing to congratulate you and your co-presenters on broadcasting the Sydney Piano Competition. It is so refreshing to hear such good music on the radio for a change. It is so much better than all that 'world music' rubbish that is too-often played.

I have read that you have been photographed in sexy underwear during a benefit for Tasmanian truck drivers. Mr. Singh has expressed a keen interest in seeing these photos. Please would you send me some copies for his Christmas stocking. I am enclosing $5 to cover the postage.

It occurs to me that all of you lady presenters on Classic FM might do a saucy Christmas calendar for charity?

Sincerely,

Mrs. Nancy Singh

ABC RADIO

ABC CLASSIC FM

ABC Classic FM
85 North East Road
Collinswood SA 5081
GPO Box 9994
Adelaide SA 5001
Tel (08) 8343 4000
Fax (08) 8343 4902

1/8/08

Dear Mrs Singh,

I think there's been some mistake!

I certainly know nothing about Tasmanian truckies, & am far too old to be posing in sexy underwear, even if the offer was there!

Sorry to disappoint, and I return your $5.

Cheers

Julian Hester

PS. Very pleased you've enjoyed S.I.P.C.A.

July 22, 2008

Mr. Wayne Swan MP
Treasurer

NANCY SINGH (MRS)
PO Box 5067
South Murwillimbah
New South Wales 2484
Import and Export Services

Dear Mr. Swan,

Many congratulations on your successful budget speech which, allowing for one or two minor errors, came over really well. I am looking forward to lower petrol prices as these affect my bottom line. When do you think the increase in interest rates will produce a fall in prices at the bowser?

It is also good to see you taking on Mr. Malcolm Turnbull who knows as much about inflation as Heather Mills about chastity belts.

I hope you will not mind my asking for a signed photograph of you. In these inflationary times I know that every penny matters, so here is $5 for the postage. I am OK, I don't have a mortgage so am doing nicely from the interest rates. Bless you!

Sincerely,

Mrs. Nancy Singh

Wayne Swan MP MEMBER FOR LILLEY

WS:LR

Mrs Nancy Singh
PO Box 5067
South Murwillimbah
NSW QLD 2484

Dear ~~Mrs Singh~~ Mrs Singh

Thank you for your letter and kind words of congratulations on our first Budget. I have enclosed a copy of my first Budget Speech along with the Budget overview that I thought you may appreciate.

The price of petrol at the bowser is influenced by many factors both nationally and internationally. The National FuelWatch Scheme is one key element of the Rudd Government's response to the rising price of petrol. We want to give motorists a fair go at the bowser. However, no government policy can guarantee that petrol prices will always go down. But FuelWatch will ensure that drivers don't pay one cent more than they have to when filling up at the bowser.

The National FuelWatch Scheme will cost $20.9 million over four years and once legislation is past the planned start date is 15 December 2008.

Thank you for taking the time to write to me and I hope the signed photo meets with your approval.

Yours sincerely

Wayne Swan
Federal Member for Lilley
Federal Treasurer

P O Box 182
Nundah QLD 4012
T 07 3266 8244 · **F** 073266 4263
E Wayne.Swan.MP@aph.gov.au
W www.SwanMP.org

July 22, 2008

NANCY SINGH (MRS)
PO Box 5067
South Murwillimbah
New South Wales 2484
Import and Export Services

Mr. Malcolm Turnbull MP

Dear Mr. Turnbull,

I am writing to congratulate you on your success in exposing Mr. Wayne Swan as an economic imbecile. He knows less about economics than a Kashmiri taxi driver.

I also watched your talk at the National Press Club a few weeks ago. It was very good. I couldn't help notice, however, that a blonde journalist – mature but still attractive – kept flirting with you. She was batting her eyelids, flicking her hair, crossing and uncrossing her legs. I am dismayed that you, a future leader of this country, should encourage such a wanton display.

I was wondering if you would please send me a signed photograph of your good self, and am enclosing $5 to cover postage.

Sincerely,

Mrs. Nancy Singh

July 22, 2008

NANCY SINGH (MRS)
PO Box 5067
South Murwillimbah
New South Wales 2484
Import and Export Services

Miss Penny Wong
Senator

Dear Senator Wong,

I am writing to say I found it difficult to understand your article on an Emissions Trading Scheme in last week's newspaper. Mind you, I was reading outside in this lovely weather we are having and a gust of wind blew up. My copy of your article and other rubbish was blown all over the place. I suppose this must be a sign.

I have heard that you are going to release your speech on green paper. What a good idea, gets the message across. Please would you send me a copy. I am enclosing $5 to cover the postage.

Sincerely,

Mrs. Nancy Singh

Australian Government

Department of Climate Change

C08/19311

Mrs Nancy Singh
PO Box 5067
MURWILLUMBAH SOUTH NSW 2484

Dear Mrs Singh

Thank you for your letter of 22 July 2008 to the Minister for Climate Change and Water, Senator the Hon Penny Wong, requesting a copy of the Minister's speech on Carbon Pollution Reduction Scheme Green Paper. I have been asked to respond.

Please find enclosed a copy of the Green Paper speech and some fact sheets that relate to the Carbon Pollution Reduction Scheme.

Also enclosed is the $5 that you sent as the postage will be covered by the Department of Climate Change.

You will find further information on climate change, or on how to make a submission to the Green Paper, on our website: www.climatechange.gov.au.

Yours sincerely

Vicki Kapernick

Vicki Kapernick
Director Communication & Stakeholder Relations
Department of Climate Change
31 July 2008

Enc

GPO Box 854, Canberra ACT 2601 Tel 02 6274 1888 Fax 02 6274 1666
www.climatechange.gov.au

July 25, 2008

NANCY SINGH (MRS)
PO Box 5067
South Murwillimbah
New South Wales 2484
Import and Export Services

Miss Anna Bligh
Premier
Queensland

Dear Miss Bligh,

I am writing to say how pleased I am to see you standing up to nasty men who put offensive slogans on the sides of vans. Words such as 'Women are like banks – once you withdraw you lose interest' or 'If God was a woman sperm would taste like chocolate', are demeaning to women and should not be tolerated. Sperm tastes nothing like chocolate, as we all know.

I am not so bothered with the slogan 'Save a Whale – Harpoon a Jap' as the Japs have always been cruel to whales and prisoners of war. They also smell of raw fish.

I hope you will not mind my asking for a signed photograph of you. In these inflationary times I know that every penny matters, so here is $5 for the postage.

Sincerely,

Mrs. Nancy Singh

July 25, 2008

Senator Mary Jo Fisher

NANCY SINGH (MRS)
PO Box 5067
South Murwillimbah
New South Wales 2484
Import and Export Services

Dear Senator Fisher,

I am very interested in providing you with advice on policy/communications as asked for in the newspaper. This is very important indeed.

I am good at researching magazines, listening to the radio and keeping abreast of politics on TV. I have very good oral skills. I have run many businesses over the years, so am used to working under pressure. I can start right away.

Sincerely,

Mrs. Nancy Singh

Mary Jo Fisher
Liberal Senator for South Australia

Ground Floor, 75 Hindmarsh Square, Adelaide SA 5000
T: 08 8223 1757 or 1300 857 022 · F: 08 8223 1750
E: senator.fisher@aph.gov.au

25 August 2008

Mrs Nancy Singh
PO Box 5067
SOUTH MURWILLIMBAH NSW 2484

Dear Nancy

Thank you for your recent application for a position in my office.

My office undertook to keep you informed regarding the recruiting process. I am still in the process of considering applications I received.

Over the coming weeks (noting that Federal Parliament sits in Canberra for four weeks out of the next five) I will arrange to interview a selection of applicants.

I shall contact you again in the future.

Yours sincerely

Senator Mary Jo Fisher
Senator for South Australia

Senator MJ

Mary Jo Fisher
Liberal Senator for South Australia

Ground Floor, 75 Hindmarsh Square, Adelaide SA 5000
T: 08 8223 1757 or 1300 857 022 · F: 08 8223 1750
E: senator.fisher@aph.gov.au

31 October 2008

Mrs Nancy Singh
PO Box 5067
SOUTH MURWILLIMBAH NSW 2484

Dear Nancy

Thank you for your recent application for a position in my office.

I am sorry that on this occasion, you've been unsuccessful.

Thank you for your interest and I wish you well in your future endeavours.

Yours sincerely

Mary Jo Fisher
Liberal Senator for South Australia

Senator MJ

July 26, 2008

Mr. Stephen Smith
Minister for Foreign Affairs

NANCY SINGH (MRS)
PO Box 5067
South Murwillimbah
New South Wales 2484
Import and Export Services

Dear Mr. Smith,

I am writing to congratulate you on managing to get in to see Condoleeza Rice during her stopover in Perth. Is she as gorgeous in person as on the small screen? You certainly looked like the cat that had got the cream!

It is strange, don't you agree, that for all the vilification of George Bush by the left and the ALP that he should have a black woman as his Secretary of State. It must be some clever bit of racism.

I hope you will not mind my asking for a signed photograph of you and Dr. Rice. In these inflationary times I know that every penny matters, so here is $5 for the postage.

Sincerely,

Mrs. Nancy Singh

Stephen Smith

August '08

August 4, 2008

His Holiness the Archbishop of Canterbury

NANCY SINGH (MRS)
PO Box 5067
South Murwillimbah
New South Wales 2484
Import and Export Services

Dear Archbishop,

I writing to say I share your frustration that everyone these days is a homosexual or a nutty Muslim. But I am not sure that letting such people – and sundry lesbians – take over the English Church is the answer to falling church attendance 'He who sups with the devil should keep his back to the wall' as the old scripture says.

The Pope is visiting Sydney soon to apologise to victims of homosexuality. I should hate to see you having to do the same. There is a lot of it about here in Australia, as in England.

I was wondering if you would send me a signed photograph of your good self, and am enclosing $5 to cover the postage. God bless you.

Sincerely,

Mrs. Nancy Singh

LAMBETH PALACE

Mr Andrew Nunn
Correspondence Secretary to the Archbishop of Canterbury

Mrs Nancy Singh
PO Box 5067
South Murwillimbah
New South Wales 2484
AUSTRALIA

Our Ref: 65858
12 August 2008

Dear Mrs Singh,

The Archbishop is now on leave after the Lambeth Conference. I am therefore writing on his behalf to thank you for your 12 July 4 August letter, both of which arrived during or in the aftermath of the Lambeth Conference. I am sorry therefore that there has been a delay in replying.

Many of those who have written to the Archbishop recently about homosexuality have made sensible contributions to the current debate. The Archbishop is grateful to them for that. He has been saddened however by the tone of some others who have written, in openly hostile and at times personal terms. Dr Williams particularly regrets the comments of those who mistakenly confuse homosexuality with paedophilia.

The Archbishop is under no illusions about the challenge posed for the Church and the Communion by the wide range of views held on these issues nor about how strongly they are held by many people. Once again, thank you for your own contribution.

I am sorry that Dr Williams' absence now makes it impossible for him to sign a photograph for you, and I herewith return the money you sent with your letter.

Yours sincerely

August 4, 2008

NANCY SINGH (MRS)
PO Box 5067
South Murwillimbah
New South Wales 2484
Import and Export Services

Mr. Boris Johnson
Lord Mayor of London

Dear Mr. Johnson

I am writing to say how sorry I am that you have had to sack two of your *aides-de-camp*. These days it is hard to tell who is homosexual and who is not. It is unusual for a black man to be homosexual, but not alas to be dodgy in financial matters. I remember the days of Stonebridge Park and Red Ken shoveling money to the West Indians, some of whom skedaddled with the lucre.

Now that I live in Australia, I can advise you that most of the men here are also homosexual, so I am not too surprised on that score. Mr. Singh says you should take on some Hindus as we have no homosexuals and we know all the tricks the Mohammedans get up to.

I hope this advice is helpful to you. I am enclosing $5 to cover postage as I should be most grateful if you would send me a signed photo of your charming self.

Sincerely,

Mrs. Nancy Singh

GREATER**LONDON**AUTHORITY

Public Liaison Unit

City Hall
The Queen's Walk
More London
London SE1 2AA
Switchboard: 020 7983 4000
Minicom: 020 7983 4458
Web: www.london.gov.uk

Mrs Singh
PO Box 5067
South Murwillimbah
New South Wales 2484
Australia

Our ref: MGLA140808-3253

Date: 5 September 2008

Dear Mrs Singh,

Whilst your comments have been noted, I must advise that the Greater London Authority is committed to promoting equality of opportunity and diversity for all in London, as well as challenging discrimination.

Please find enclosed the $5.00 sent to the Mayor of London, which I am returning as we are unable to accept cash.

Yours sincerely,

Alison Turner

Alison Turner
Public Services Co-ordinator

Direct telephone: 020 7983 4100 Fax: 020 7983 4057 Email: mayor@london.gov.uk

August 6, 2008

NANCY SINGH (MRS)
PO Box 5067
South Murwillimbah
New South Wales 2484
Import and Export Services

Mr. Alan Carpenter
Premier
Western Australia

Dear Mr. Carpenter,

I am writing to congratulate you on your decision to crack down on violent crime. At last the far left are admitting they were wrong all of these years. I look forward to reading of much harsher punishments *pour encourager des autres.*

Mr. Singh and I were forced to leave Britain because Tony Blair allowed violent crime to spiral out of control. Even his wife is now complaining that the streets are not safe; while government ministers these days wear 'stab vests'. Much of the violence was, of course, started by the blacks, but now the white trash are joining in. On top of this, Britain is full of nutty Muslim suicide bombers.

I am sending you a copy of a wonderful article on the Scottish judge who ended the razor gangs in Glasgow in the 1950s. He seems to have had the right idea.

Perhaps we could even bring back public flogging? I am all in favour of this and so am sending $5 as a contribution to your campaign fund. Go get them!

Sincerely,

Mrs. Nancy Singh

Department of the **Premier and Cabinet**
Government of **Western Australia**

Office of the **Director General**

Our Ref: 200807004
Enquiries: Telephone (08) 9222 9428

Mrs N Singh
PO Box 5067
SOUTH MURWILLIMBAH NSW 2484

Dear Mrs Singh

I acknowledge your letter dated 6 August, addressed to the Premier, enclosing a copy of an article from the *International Express* newspaper about Lord Carmont, who presided in Glasgow in the 1950s and gained a reputation for tough sentencing.

As a State Election is to be held on Saturday, 6 September 2008, the Government has assumed a 'caretaker' role. Given these circumstances, the Premier has asked me to reply on his behalf.

Your views about law and order have been noted and I acknowledge the $5.00 which you enclosed as a contribution towards the Premier's campaign fund.

The State Government cannot accept campaign donations and I am therefore returning the amount of $5.00. Any contributions to the Premier's election campaign fund should be forwarded directly to the Western Australian Labor Party, which is located at Unity House, 79 Stirling Street, Perth, WA, 6805.

Yours sincerely

M C Wauchope
DIRECTOR GENERAL

Enc

27 AUG 2008

197 St Georges Terrace, Perth, Western Australia 6000
Telephone: (08) 9222 9888 Facsimile: (08) 9322 1213
Email: admin@dpc.wa.gov.au
ABN 61 313 082 730

XDPCL002

August 6, 2008

NANCY SINGH (MRS)
PO Box 5067
South Murwillimbah
New South Wales 2484
Import and Export Services

Mr. Lindsay Tanner
Minister for Finance

Dear Mr. Tanner,

I must say I enjoy the sight of a big strong man talking about inflicting cuts and taking hard measures. You are absolutely right that Australia has gone too soft and there are far too many dole bums. I am pleased that government policy is at last to trigger a recession and thus exert downward pressure on employment. You should be cutting benefits too.

I hope you will not mind my asking for a signed photograph of you. In these inflationary times I know that every penny matters, so here is $5 for the postage. My investments are doing nicely thanks to high interest rates and oil prices. Thank you!

Sincerely,

Mrs. Nancy Singh

Lindsay Tanner MP
Federal Member for Melbourne
Minister for Finance and Deregulation

Friday, 29 August 2008

Mrs Nancy Singh
PO Box 5067
South Murwillimbah
NSW 2484

Dear Mrs Singh

Thanks for your letter of August 6, 2008.

I am afraid that the sentiments you attribute to me in your letter, such as seeking to trigger a recession, are not correct.

I am returning your $5. Please let me know if your request for a photo stands. If so I will be happy to forward one to you without charge.

Yours sincerely

Lindsay Tanner

Lindsay Tanner MP
Minister for Finance and Deregulation
Federal Member for Melbourne

Electorate Office: 102 Victoria Street Carlton 3053 • **Tel:** (03) 9347 5000 • **Fax:** (03) 9347 1351
Parliament House Office: Parliament House Canberra 2600 • **Tel:** (02) 6277 7400 • **Fax:** (02) 6273 4110
Email: lindsay.tanner.mp@aph.gov.au • **Website:** www.lindsaytanner.com.au

August 9, 2008

Miss Cate Blanchett
C/o Mr. Kevin Rudd MP

NANCY SINGH (MRS)
PO Box 5067
South Murwillimbah
New South Wales 2484
Import and Export Services

Dear Miss Blanchett,

I am sorry to be writing to you care of Mr. Kevin Rudd, but I know of no other way to make contact. What a nerdy little twerp, and I sympathise with your having to put up with him slobbering all over you for political gain.

I was particularly shocked to read that he made remarks about your bosoms being large enough to house a small yellow-toed rock wallaby or some other marsupial. This may be true of his wife, but he should keep such offensive remarks within his own *boudoir*.

You are a very beautiful and talented young woman and a credit to Australia. I hope you will not mind my asking for a signed photograph of you for Mr. Singh. I am enclosing $5 to cover the postage.

Sincerely,

Mrs. Nancy Singh

August 9, 2008

NANCY SINGH (MRS)
PO Box 5067
South Murwillimbah
New South Wales 2484
Import and Export Services

Mr. Gordon Brown MP
Prime Minister of the United Kingdom

Dear Mr. Brown,

I am writing to say how sorry I am that you are getting the blame for the mess Tony Blair made of Britain, especially as regards violent street crime and racial conflict, and filthy hospitals. I hope you are not worrying unduly about the common folk of Glasgow East; I stayed in Glasgow for a few months once and couldn't wait to leave again. The people there are worse than Birmingers. It is hard to believe that Scotland once produced the likes of Adam Smith, Lord Kames and David Hume.

I still believe you have what it takes to be a truly great PM in the mould of Cromwell or Walpole, or even Wellington. The trick to this is to be hard, very hard, and not to waver – cut taxes, get rid of Darling and deport (exile is probably a better words for appearances sake) several thousand Muslims. I think you should get tough with crime as did another great Scot, Lord Carmont, in the 1950s. Sacking Trevor Phillips would also be a popular move.

Although certainly no socialist, I know a good man when I see one. Watch out for Miliband, a little creep like his father – a so-called welfare economist – before him. It might be an idea to sack a few ministers to let the people know who is to blame for high taxes, too-high immigration, knife crime, loony local councils, fly-tipping and the closure of post offices. On the plus side, it is good that the populace is now transfixed with shallow vulgarity and is so poorly educated, following years of trendy education theory gone mad, that they understand very little of the great affairs of state.

Sincerely,

Mrs. Nancy Singh

10 DOWNING STREET
LONDON SW1A 2AA
www.number10.gov.uk

From the Direct Communications Unit 20 August 2008

Mrs Nancy Singh
PO Box 5067
South Murwillimbah
New South Wales 2484
Australia

Dear Mrs Singh

The Prime Minister has asked me to thank you for your recent letter.

Mr Brown appreciates your kind thought in writing.

Yours sincerely

M Davies

MR M DAVIES

August 9, 2008

Mrs. Justine Elliot
Minister for Ageing

NANCY SINGH (MRS)
PO Box 5067
South Murwillimbah
New South Wales 2484
Import and Export Services

Dear Mrs. Elliot,

I fear I may have written to you under a misapprehension. I now understand that your role in the government is not to help women look younger, important though this is to us all. If a woman looks good, she feels good.

Rather, I now understand that your task is deciding how to cope with the epidemic of old people as they prepare to shuffle off this mortal coil. I can see that in this regard it makes perfect sense to close popular small, local hospitals so that the sites can be sold to developers. A good example locally is the Murwillumbah Hospital which I now understand it is government policy to shut. The old people can then more efficiently be processed at new, large ugly hospitals accessible only by car and surrounded by a sea of car parking. This might help put a lot of them off attending, and so will cut waiting lists.

I know you are a very busy person, while I am just an ordinary member of the public, but I do hope you will find some time to reply to this letter.

Sincerely,

Mrs. Nancy Singh

Justine Elliot MP

MEMBER FOR RICHMOND

Office: 107-111 Minjungbal Drive, Tweed Heads South ▪ Mail: PO Box 6996, Tweed Heads South, NSW 2486
Email: justine.elliot.mp@aph.gov.au ▪ **Phone: (07) 5523 4371** or **1300 720 675** ▪ Fax: (07) 5523 4379

12-8-08

Dear Nancy,

Justine asked me to acknowledge receipt of your letter received in her office today. I could not locate your details on the electoral Roll, nor could I locate a telephone contact. Could you please give this office a call to discuss this further.

Regards Jodie

With Compliments

August 9, 2008

NANCY SINGH (MRS)
PO Box 5067
South Murwillimbah
New South Wales 2484
Import and Export Services

Mr. George Bush
President of the United States of America

Dear Mr. Bush,

I am writing to say that Mr. Singh and I and many others will miss you when you step down as President in January. I have always admired the fact that you stick to your guns and appreciate that you have had many difficult decisions to make. I personally feel much safer knowing that your troops are 'kicking ass' in Iraq, and I am hopeful that Iran will soon feel America's might. I am only saddened that Australia's army was not up to finishing the job in Iraq.

Dr. Condoleeza Rice was here in Australia recently, stopping over on her way somewhere more important. She met our new Foreign Minister, whose name escapes me. I know this is a bit cheeky, but could you possibly send me a photo of your good self and Dr. Rice. I like your craggy good looks, but Mr. Singh definitely prefers Dr. Rice.

Wishing you well in your retirement.

NO RESPONSE

Sincerely,

Mrs. Nancy Singh

PS – Have you noticed that Pres. Clinton these days looks like 'A Picture of Dorian Gray'?

August 9, 2008

NANCY SINGH (MRS)
PO Box 5067
South Murwillimbah
New South Wales 2484
Import and Export Services

Mrs. Harriet Harman MP
Mrs. Jacqui Smith MP
Home Secretary

Dear Mrs. Harman/Mrs. Smith,

Mr. Singh and I are making an enforced return trip to the UK to attend a family funeral in Southall. We left Britain in 1998 to get away from high taxes, black street crime and the Muslim menace. We are horrified to read of all the stabbings in London these days, although we are not in the least surprised. We are naturally worried that we might be knifed to death in broad daylight.

Mr. Singh has suggested we buy a stab-vest of the type he says you yourself wear when, unfortunately, you have to walk the streets or otherwise come into contact with the common people. Unfortunately, I have lost the newspaper clipping in which you modeled said garment. I wonder if you would be good enough to send us a copy and also to recommend a good manufacturer.

I am enclosing $5 to cover postage and would be most grateful for a speedy response as I imagine this product is in great demand.

Sincerely,

Mrs. Nancy Singh

Now you don't have to, thanks to this KEBAB VEST

"My constituents in Peckham are all murderers, so I never go anywhere near them without putting on my Viz Anti-Stab Kebab Vest first. Come to think of it, I never go to Peckham anyway, unless there's an election coming up."

Harriet Harman MP

SHRUGS OFF attacks from:

- *Dagger-wielding youths*
- *Kids in "hooded sports tops" with flick-knives*
- *Naked escaped luna-.tics brandishing Samurai swords*

INSTRUCTIONS

Cut out the front and rear vest panels and attach 2 Argos catalogues using Pritt. Attach front and back panels with string as shown in the diagram. Then, next time you go out, put it on and enjoy your kebab, safe in the knowledge that the tip of your assailant's blade is never going to make it past the patio furniture section.

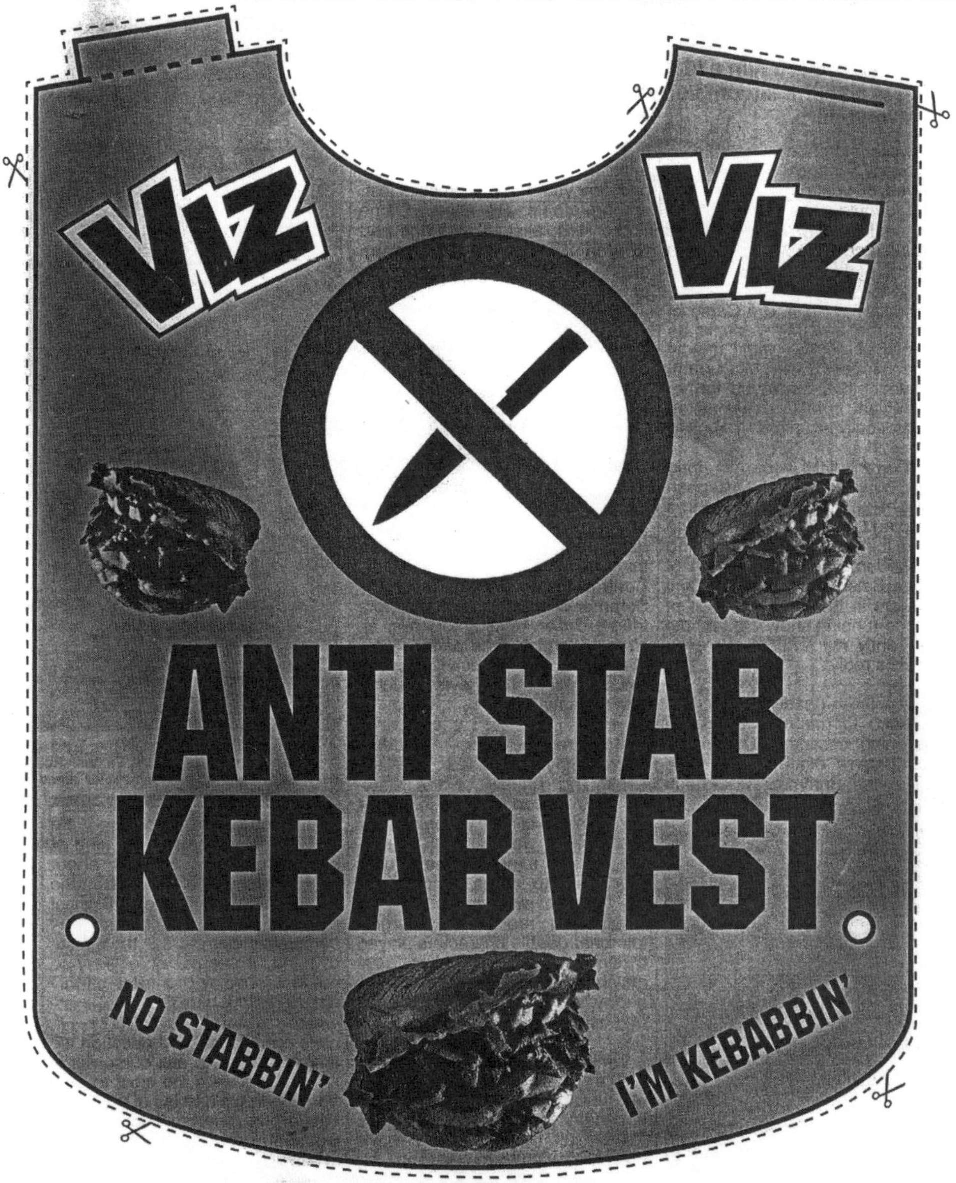

about the B VEST

hen I got stabbed much better with t."

George Harrison

ch fun. is vest

d Elliot

Nottingham me I leant out of ked potatoes and ck like that, you'd I'll be wearing my

tim Brian Harvey

hen I got teffi Graf s game,

a Seles

os of the Roman 44BC. If I'd been at fateful Ides of

te Julius Caesar

Viz Viz

ANTI STAB KEBAB VEST

NO STABBIN' I'M KEBABBIN'

Home Office

Direct Communications Unit
2 Marsham Street, London SW1P 4DF
Switchboard 020 7035 4848 Fax: 020 7035 4745 Textphone: 020 7035 4742
E-mail: public.enquiries@homeoffice.gsi.gov.uk Website: www.homeoffice.gov.uk

Mrs Nancy Singh
PO Box 5067
South Murwillimbah
New South Wales
2484

Reference: T20970/8

17 October 2008

Dear Mrs Singh,

Thank you for your letter of 12 September to the Home Secretary about not receiving a reply to your letter of 9 September. Your letter has been passed to the Direct Communications Unit and I have been asked to reply.

I am afraid that I cannot find any record of your letter with the above date. I would be grateful if you could send a copy of your original letter to enable us to provide you with an appropriate response. Once we receive your letter, we will endeavour to send you a response within 20 working days.

I thank you for contacting the Home Office.

Yours sincerely,

M. Lock

Mrs M Lockmun
Direct Communications Unit

August 9, 2008

NANCY SINGH (MRS)
PO Box 5067
South Murwillimbah
New South Wales 2484
Import and Export Services

Mr. Trevor Phillips
Chairman
Equalities Commission

Dear Mr. Phillips,

I am writing to say how much I agree with your comments that Britain is 'hideously and disgustingly white'. The white working classes are particularly over-represented, thick and ignorant.

Mind you, the blacks have a lot to answer for too, running around London knifing each other. Mr. Singh and I left Britain in the late 1990s to get away from Tony Blair, high taxes and black crime.

The worst of the lot of course are the fanatical Muslims who are not happy unless they are blowing up public transport, which I myself never use any more. Mr. Singh predicts a Muslim takeover of Birmingham, along the lines of Kosovo, within ten years.

I hope this information is helpful to you, forewarned is forearmed. However, I suspect that it is too late, even for you as head of the race relations industry, to do much about it. I am enclosing $5 to cover postage costs as I should be most grateful if you would send me a signed photo of your charming self.

Sincerely,

Mrs. Nancy Singh

Equality and
Human Rights
Commission

equalityhumanrights.com

Mrs Nancy Singh
PO Box 5067
Murwillimbah
New South Wales 2484

Our ref: TP/KG/237Singh
Date: 18 August 2008

Further to your letter of 9 August 2008 I am returning your $5 note, as Mr Phillips does not provide signed photographs.

Yours sincerely

Karen Grayson
Policy Adviser to the Chair

Equality and
Human Rights
Commission

3 More London Riverside
Tooley Street
London SE1 2RG

Tel: 0203 117 0235
Fax: 020 7407 7557
info@equalityhumanrights.com

August 9, 2008

Miss Tanya Plibersek
Minister for Housing

NANCY SINGH (MRS)
PO Box 5067
South Murwillimbah
New South Wales 2484
Import and Export Services

Dear Miss Plibersek,

Further to my letter of 8th Inst. I am writing to say that I had not taken you for the sort of woman who pockets small sums intended to cover post and packing. I realise that you are a Very Important Person and I am just a member of a hardworking Australian family, but I did expect better from a people's representative.

Sincerely,

Mrs. Nancy Singh

Australian Government

Department of Families, Housing, Community Services and Indigenous Affairs

PO Box 7576 Canberra Business Centre
ACT 2610
Telephone 1300 653 227
TTY 1800 260 402
Facsimile
E-mail
www.fahcsia.gov.au

MC08-022773

Mrs Nancy Singh
PO Box 5067
SOUTH MURWILLUMBAH NSW 2484

20 AUG 2008

Dear Mrs Singh

Thank you for your letter of 8 July 2008 to the Minister for Housing, the Hon Tanya Plibersek MP. The Minister has asked me to reply on her behalf.

The Minister appreciates your support and the time you have taken to write to her. I am returning your $5 and as requested have enclosed a photograph of Minister Plibersek.

Once again, thank you for writing.

Yours sincerely

Ministerial and Parliamentary Services

Encl.

August 9, 2008

Miss Nicola Roxon MP
Minister for Health

NANCY SINGH (MRS)
PO Box 5067
South Murwillimbah
New South Wales 2484
Import and Export Services

Dear Miss Roxon,

I am very disappointed not to have received a response to my letter of the 8th Inst., and I am sure you will agree that even an idiot can see that your policy of putting up the price of alcopops is a complete failure. I know you are very important and I am just a member of a hard-working Australian family, but I did expect some common courtesy.

Well, never mind all that now. I have noticed that it is not only groceries and petrol that fluctuate wildly in price from store to store, but also wine. I put it to you that the government should introduce a *WineWatch* scheme to complement *GroceryWatch* and *FuelWatch*. True, such initiatives cause old people to drive about and queue all day to save a few dollars, causing traffic congestion. But at least it gives them something to do other than stuffing their faces and watching plasma televisions all day.

Sincerely,

Mrs. Nancy Singh

Australian Government

Department of Health and Ageing

Mrs Nancy Singh
PO Box 5067
SOUTH MURWILLIMBAH NSW 2484

Dear Mrs Singh

Thank you for your recent correspondence to the Minister for Health and Ageing, the Hon Nicola Roxon concerning alcohol issues. This matter falls within the portfolio responsibility of the Parliamentary Secretary for Health and Ageing, Senator the Hon Jan McLucas. The Parliamentary Secretary has asked me to reply on her behalf.

On 14 March 2008, the Prime Minister announced a National Binge Drinking Strategy which provides $53.5 million to address binge drinking among young people. This includes:

- $14.4 million to invest in community level initiatives to confront the culture of binge drinking, particularly in sporting organisations;
- $19.1 million to intervene earlier to assist young people and ensure that they assume personal responsibility for their binge drinking; and
- $20 million to fund advertising that confronts young people with the costs and consequences of binge drinking.

At the Council of Australian Governments (COAG) meeting on 26 March 2008, it was agreed to ask the Ministerial Council on Drug Strategy (MCDS) to develop options to reduce binge drinking including the secondary supply of alcohol to teenagers, responsible service of alcohol, operating hours for licensed venues and the alcohol content of ready-to-drink alcohol beverages. COAG also asked the Australia and New Zealand Food Regulation Ministerial Council to request Food Standards Australia New Zealand to consider mandatory health warnings on packaged alcohol.

Subsequently, on 23 May 2008, the MCDS agreed to expand the report to COAG to include an assessment of the effectiveness of existing and trial late night lockout arrangements across the States and Territories and standards and controls for alcohol advertising targeting young people.

MCDS will provide an interim report for consideration in October 2008, before preparing a final report to COAG in December 2008.

In addition, the Australian Government has announced a change to alcohol excise rates so that all spirit-based drinks, whether pre-mixed or unmixed, will pay the same rate of excise. This decision will increase the excise on pre-mixed alcohol beverages by approximately 70%,

Drug Strategy Branch MDP 27 GPO Box 9848 Canberra ACT 2601
Telephone: 02 6289 8771 Fax: 02 6289 7837 ABN 83 605 426 759

raising the cost of these products by up to $1.30 per container. Many research studies have shown that higher prices lead to a reduction in demand, particularly for young people.

As a result, a substantial amount of funding raised from the increase in the excise rate on spirit-based drinks will be directed to the Government's preventative health care agenda. Government programs to control alcohol misuse are not limited to the taxation of alcohol products but constitute a balanced package of measures including public education and information campaigns, community prevention initiatives and treatment programs.

Announced by the Minister for Health and Ageing, the Hon Nicola Roxon MP, on 9 April 2008, the Preventative Health Taskforce will develop the National Preventative Health Strategy as a blueprint for tackling the burden of chronic disease currently caused by obesity, tobacco and excessive consumption of alcohol.

In developing the Strategy, the taskforce is consulting widely with experts from across the health care sector and the broader community. It will release a discussion paper in September 2008 that will set out a framework for the Strategy and key issues. A draft of the Strategy will then be released for comment in March 2009 before the finalised Strategy itself is handed to the Government in June 2009.

I trust that the above information is of use.

Yours sincerely

V Hart

Virginia Hart
Assistant Secretary
Drug Strategy Branch
15 September 2008

August 9, 2008

Mr. Glenn Stevens,
Governor of the Federal Reserve Bank

NANCY SINGH (MRS)
PO Box 5067
South Murwillimbah
New South Wales 2484
Import and Export Services

Dear Mr. Stevens,

Further to my letter of the 8th Inst., I am dismayed not to have received a reply. I realise you are a Very Important Person and I am just an ordinary member of the public, but I did expect the common decency of a reply. I am after all a taxpayer and therefore, indirectly, your employer.

It is now plain for all to see that economists in Federal Banks are a bunch of imbeciles, starting with Messrs Greenspan and Bernanke who caused all this by stupidly putting up interest rates in 2005 and 2006. They should have left well enough alone, as most of the 'inflation' we now have is either self-correcting or is not responsive to interest rate variations. This, I am sure you now realise, explains why the economy is stalling and yet the official inflation rate is today higher than it was a year ago.

In the circumstances I fear you must fall on your sword.

Sincerely,

Mrs. Nancy Singh

RESERVE BANK OF AUSTRALIA

65 MARTIN PLACE
SYDNEY NSW 2000
PHONE: (61 2) 9551 9507
FAX: (61 2) 9551 8030
EMAIL: governor@rba.gov.au

G.R. Stevens
GOVERNOR

13 August 2008

Mrs Nancy Singh
PO Box 5067
SOUTH MURWILLUMBAH NSW 2484

Dear Mrs Singh,

I did receive your letter of 9 August 2008, but I found its tone to be rather sarcastic and so I wasn't sure what response I could offer.

Your second letter suggests that central banks are wrong to raise interest rates to control inflation, and that somehow inflation will be self correcting. I rather doubt that the pressure on prices which has been so widespread, in an environment of exceptionally strong growth in demand, would have been sorted out quite so easily as that. In Australia, growth in demand in the economy ran, in 2007, at a pace nearly twice the rate at which the economy's potential capacity to supply could expand. Demand had to slow if inflation is to be corrected. It now has. Inflation will, in my judgment, decline gradually over time, but that will occur with a lag. It always does.

You state that Messrs Greenspan, Bernanke and others are imbeciles. Knowing both men and having participated in discussions with them numerous times, I'm afraid I will have to differ with you on that as well.

Yours sincerely,

August 9, 2008

Miss Penny Wong,
Senator

NANCY SINGH (MRS)
PO Box 5067
South Murwillimbah
New South Wales 2484
Import and Export Services

Dear Senator Wong,

Some well-intentioned person in your office, a Miss Kapernick, very kindly replied to my letter of 27th Inst., enclosing the government's policy on 'Carbon Pollution Reduction'. I had asked for the version Emissions Trading Scheme printed on green paper.

I am surprised to learn that carbon is a pollutant. I had always believed it to be a natural element, and that plants and trees breathe in carbon dioxide. Is it really the case that carbon is a pollutant?

I think it is wonderful that you as a non-white woman should be in such an important position. You are an inspiration to all we ethnics.

Sincerely,

Mrs. Nancy Singh

August 9, 2008

SYNOPSIS: An Undercover Life

A Novel by Nancy Singh

NANCY SINGH (MRS)
PO Box 5067
South Murwillimbah
New South Wales 2484
Import and Export Services

Slim, tanned and elegant, Maria Armitraj stretches in her luxurious king size bed. Still young-looking and attractive, she reflects happily on her life and her many possessions. Mind you, it was hard work getting here! She has come a long way since, as a nine-year-old in 1958, she was forced into service in Che Guevera's personal harem. How she survived his monstrous temper and deviant sexual appetites astounds her to this day. She was lucky enough to meet a bi-sexual Roman Catholic priest from Adelaide. He helped her to escape from Cuba, and they spent many years travelling South America together during which time he taught her how to pleasure a man. Recalled to Adelaide – 'City of Churches and Axe Murderers' – she accompanied Father Don, as his housekeeper. On his death from a rare strain of hepatitis, she left backward Adelaide for Canberra where for 30 years she ran a successful gentleman's club and escort agency, catering mainly to politicians. To begin with she had to work long hours herself before taking on Vietnamese staff in the 70s.

She smiles as she remembers some of her old clients: Troika the Treasurer, the Premier's 'Club Sandwich', the transvestite judges and bottom-fancying civil servants. What tales she could tell!

She stretches once more and begins her daily pelvic floor exercises. It is important for her to remain firm, not to end up like a wizard's sleeve. Now that she has hooked Mr. Armitraj, the banana magnate, it is important to keep him happy for another two years before she can arrange a lucrative divorce.

She smiles to herself, it all began a long time ago …

Sincerely,

Mrs. Nancy Singh

HarperCollins*Publishers*
Pty Limited
ABN 36 009 913 517

25 Ryde Road (P.O. Box 321)
Pymble NSW 2073
Australia

Telephone (02) 9952 5409
Facsimile (02) 9952 5444
Lucie.crowhurst@harpercollins.com.au

A NEWS CORPORATION COMPANY

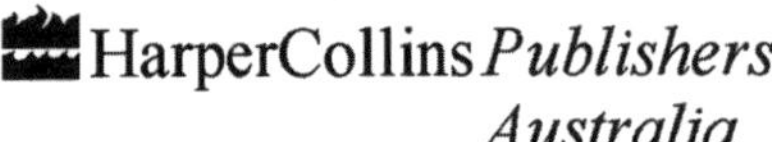

18 August, 2008

Mrs. Nancy Singh,
PO Box 5067,
South Murwillumbah, 2484

Dear Mrs. Singh,

Referring to your letter dated 9/8/08 enclosing a synopsis of your manuscript *An Undercover Life*. Unfortunately we are no longer considering unsolicited manuscripts for publication.

We wish you every success in finding a suitable publisher and thank you for your interest in approaching HarperCollins.

Yours sincerely,

Lucie Crowhurst
Editorial Administration.

Friday, 12 September 2008

ABC Ultimo Centre
700 Harris Street
Ultimo NSW 2007

GPO Box 9994
Sydney NSW 2001

Tel. +61 2 8333 1500
abc.net.au

Nancy Singh
PO Box 5067
South Murwillimbah NSW 2484

Re An Undercover Life

Dear Nancy Singh

Thank you for giving ABC Books the opportunity to consider your book proposal. We have looked at it with interest but, unfortunately, we don't think we have a place for it in our list.

We wish you every success in your search for a publisher.

Yours sincerely

Brigitta Doyle
ABC Books
GPO Box 9994
Sydney NSW 2001
P 8333 3963
F 8333 3888

HARLEQUIN MILLS & BOON
LIMITED

Dear Nancy,

Thank you for sending your submission and for your patience in awaiting our response.
* Synopsis

Harlequin Mills & boon deal exclusively with the genre of romantic fiction for woman. Since you material does not come into this category, we are unable to offer an opinion on your work.

Thank you for thinking of Harlequin Mills & Boon.

Yours sincerely

Editorial Department
Harlequin Mills & Boon

August 14, 2008

Mr. Chris Bowen MP
Minister for Grocery Prices

NANCY SINGH (MRS)
PO Box 5067
South Murwillimbah
New South Wales 2484
Import and Export Services

Dear Mr. Bowen,

I am writing to say how charming and self-effacing you came across on TV when pretending not to know the price of a loaf of bread or a carton of milk.

That said, I have noticed that it is not only groceries and petrol that fluctuate wildly in price from store to store but also wine. I put it to you that the government should introduce a *WineWatch* scheme to complement *GroceryWatch* and *FuelWatch*. True, such initiatives cause old people to drive about and queue all day to save a few dollars, causing traffic congestion. But at least it gives them something to do other than stuffing their faces and watching plasma televisions all day.

Sincerely,

Mrs. Nancy Singh

August 14, 2008

Mr. Phillip Adams
Writer and Broadcaster

Dear Mr. Adams,

I am writing to ask your advice on a sensitive matter. Mr. Singh has announced he intends to enter politics. He says the pension would come in handy as we approach old age. He is opting for the ALP as they are currently in power.

The problem for me is that there appears to be a very strong correlation between left-wing politics and men cheating on their wives. President Kennedy, for example, was a satyr on steroids who instructed his bodyguards to procure 3 women a day for him. He also had an affair with Marilyn Monroe, who later died in unusual circumstances. Bill Clinton spilled his seed all over poor Monica Lewinsky and lied about it under oath. Now we have John Edwards siring a child by a mistress and then denying it. Here at home we had Bob Hawke jumping from bed to bed, and then the awful Mr. Keating leaving his wife for a slattern. As far as I can tell, John Howard never behaved in this way, nor did dreary old Malcolm Fraser. I'm not sure about Whitlam. Neither of the Bush presidents is an adulterer, and old Reagan divorced his first wife before his affair with Nancy. Mrs. Thatcher certainly never had an affair! But on the left even soppy Tony Blair was at it with Caroline Chaplin.

I was wondering if you would be able to confirm my theory? It would be a great help to me in keeping Mr. Singh on the path of virtue. Besides, he is much too intelligent to waste his time on politics.

NANCY SINGH (MRS)
PO Box 5067
South Murwillimbah
New South Wales 2484
Import and Export Services

Would you please also send me a signed photograph of your good self? I am enclosing $5 to cover postage in these inflationary times.

Sincerely,

Mrs. Nancy Singh

PHILLIP ADAMS

3 September 2008

Mrs Nancy Singh
PO Box 5067
South Murwillimbah
NSW 2484

Dear Nancy

How appalling! Mr Singh's intention to enter politics. Please advise him that it would be far better to enter a monastery. Though that's probably forbidden by your ethnic and religious connections.

You're perfectly right. As soon as one becomes a left-wing politician the trousers head due south. Even if you're a left-wing politician in thin conservative disguise, like Malcolm Fraser, the dacks drop. Particularly in proximity to Memphis.

Bill Clinton, Bob Hawke, Jack Kennedy – the list goes on and on. The only significant polititican I know who's strictly observed his marriage vows has been Paul Keating. The only thing that can be said in their favour is that, by and large, we're discussing heterosexuality rather than the abominable crime of buggery. This is, of course, much more popular in monasteries.

I think the Chinese got it right during imperial times. Placing eunuchs in high positions was a very good tactic.

That's the trouble with circumcision. They don't take it far enough.

Best wishes

Phil xx

PHILLIP ADAMS

I attach a pic of myself as Pope Innocent XI which I have signed on the back.

PHILLIP ADAMS AO
ELMSWOOD GUNDY NSW 2337
FAX (02) 9362 3971
philadams@ozemail.com.au

August 14, 2008

NANCY SINGH (MRS)
PO Box 5067
South Murwillimbah
New South Wales 2484
Import and Export Services

Mr. Damien Beaumont
Classic FM
ABC Radio

Dear Mr. Beaumont,

I am writing to say how much I am enjoying the BBC Proms series broadcast from London. We have so much to thank the English for!

However, on Tuesday 12th I distinctly heard the announcer say, at the end of the concert, 'And now the orchestra is flanking her behind'. I am sure this was just a miss-speak in the heat of the moment, rather than an attempt at modern so-called humour?

Keep up the excellent work.

Sincerely,

Mrs. Nancy Singh

22 August 2008

Mrs Nancy Singh
PO Box 5067
South Murwillimbah, NSW 2484

ABC Ultimo Centre
700 Harris Street
Ultimo NSW 2007
GPO Box 9994
Sydney NSW 2001
Tel. +61 2 8333 1500
abc.net.au

Dear Mrs Singh,

Thank you for your letter dated August 14, 2008 regarding the BBC Proms broadcast on August 12. We are extremely pleased to hear you are enjoying the broadcast.

I have listened back to the recording of the broadcast you mentioned, and you are correct. The presenter did in fact say that the London Sinfonietta was flanking her behind. I am sure this was a mis-speak on behalf of the presenter in the pressure of presenting such a high profile and exciting concert. I cannot confirm that for sure, as it was a BBC presenter.

Thank you once again for your enthusiasm of the broadcast and your loyalty and support to ABC Classic FM and the wider ABC.

Yours sincerely,

Lucas Burns
Assistant to Manager
ABC Classic FM
Direct line 02 8333 2693

Singh N 220808 Proms

August 14, 2008

NANCY SINGH (MRS)
PO Box 5067
South Murwillimbah
New South Wales 2484
Import and Export Services

Miss Julia Gillard MP
Minister for Productivity, Education and Socialism

Dear Miss Gillard,

I watched your interview on *Insiders* last Sunday with great interest. I think you made an excellent defence of *FuelWatch* and *GroceryWatch*. However, the prospect of people 'getting in and out of their cars' to hunt down 'specials' is not one I view with much enthusiasm.

About 15 years ago Mr. Singh and I lived in the West of England. Honestly, the roads were almost completely clogged with old people driving about for want of anything better to do. They would fill up on petrol at a certain garage every Tuesday, go to Aldi for meat on Mondays, buy their lavatory supplies on a Wednesday and shop for fish on a Thursday. The rest of the time they drive about trying to find the cheapest drug prescriptions. I shudder to think how much petrol is consumed in this way, how many emissions are the result of old people shopping for 'good deals'.

On a more positive note, I thought you looked very bonny on Sunday. Your make-up was very good, and I like your new hairstyle. I wonder if you would be willing to send a signed photo to Mr. Singh as he thinks you are a feisty one. I am enclosing $5 to cover postage.

Sincerely,

Mrs. Nancy Singh

August 14, 2008

NANCY SINGH (MRS)
PO Box 5067
South Murwillimbah
New South Wales 2484
Import and Export Services

Mr. Kevin Rudd MP
Prime Minister

Dear Mr. Rudd,

I am disappointed that you have been too busy to reply to my letter of 8th Inst. I know that you have been out of the country a lot, but I had not taken you for the sort of chap who would pocket $5 meant for postage.

I read your comments on von Hayek's *The Road to Serfdom.* I was greatly surprised at your misreading of this great work, and your apparent ignorance of history as well as economics. It alarms me that you appear to think the State knows best. Of course, as a China enthusiast you are probably more sympathetic to communism than ordinary sensible people. I was wondering if you believe that a version of Chinese Communism would be good for Australia, and is this why you are so keen on a EU-style Asian Union? Would it become compulsory to have only one child (to cut down carbon emissions) and to eat duck's feet?

Since it seems you are not willing to send me a signed photograph of you as requested, could I please have my $5 back …

Sincerely,

Mrs. Nancy Singh

August 27, 2008

His Holiness the Archbishop of Canterbury

NANCY SINGH (MRS)
PO Box 5067
South Murwillimbah
New South Wales 2484
Import and Export Services

Dear Your Worhipfulness,

Some well-meaning admin assistant in your office replied to my recent letter to you. He points out that there is a distinction to be made between homosexuals and pedophiles. This is of course true, although it does seem that rather a large proportion of pedophiles are homosexual. The latest case here in Australia involves a Catholic priest and 33 young boys.

Such a distinction can also be made between men marrying men as opposed to other women. Surely if God went to the trouble to make women, He did not intend men to use each other's bottoms for sexual purposes?

I hope the Church will return to looking after the flock, that is children, normal men and women and families. God bless you.

Sincerely,

Mrs. Nancy Singh

August 27, 2008

Senator Bob Brown,

NANCY SINGH (MRS)
PO Box 5067
South Murwillimbah
New South Wales 2484
Import and Export Services

Dear Mr. Brown,

I am writing to ask your advice on a sensitive matter of conscience. Mr. Singh and I are committed to saving the planet as much as the next person. We like to buy a new car every two years to keep abreast of technological developments and fuel-efficient engines. Normally we buy a Mercedes, an Audi, or a BMW, but this year these cars are facing a hike in so-called 'luxury car tax'.

I am wondering if you know which models are currently the best for the environment, perhaps the very car that you yourself drive? Any advice would be much appreciated.

I was hoping you would please send me a signed photograph of your good self, and am enclosing $5 to cover postage.

Sincerely,

Mrs. Nancy Singh

Australian Senate

Bob Brown
Australian Greens Senator for Tasmania

2 Sept 2008

Mrs Nancy Singh
PO Box 5067
South Murwillimbah NSW 2484

Dear Nancy,

Thank you for writing to Senator Brown; his hectic schedule prevents him from personally replying.

I commend you for seeking information from Bob about which car is most fuel-efficient, however, neither this office, nor Senator Brown are in a position to recommend a particular vehicle for you.

For your information, rather than by way of endorsement, Bob drives a Toyota Prius. I would urge you to contact a consumer advocacy organisation such as *Choice* for advice about vehicle efficiency.

Unfortunately Senator Brown is unable to provide an autographed photo of himself, and I am returning the $5 that you sent with your letter.

Kind regards,

Anna Sildever
Office of Senator Bob Brown

www.bobbrown.org.au

August 27, 2008

Director of TV Entertainment
ABC

NANCY SINGH (MRS)
PO Box 5067
South Murwillimbah
New South Wales 2484
Import and Export Services

Dear Sir,

I have noticed that the jokes told on ABC light entertainment shows such as *Enough Rope* are simply not very funny. Also there is far too much sexual innuendo and nods towards the dark side of homosexuality. This suggests you perhaps need some new scriptwriters.

In order to get the ball rolling, here are two favourite jokes of Mr. Singh and I:

> 'A man walks into the pub, sees his friend sitting at the bar and walks up to him. His friend says 'your round' and he replies 'so are you, you fat bastard.' Ho Ho!
>
> 'I know a man with one leg called Fred.'
> 'What's the name of his other leg?'
> 'That's a matter of a pinion.'

My invoice for this material will follow in a day or so.

Sincerely,

Mrs. Nancy Singh

August 27, 2008

Prof. Tim Flannery,

NANCY SINGH (MRS)
PO Box 5067
South Murwillimbah
New South Wales 2484
Import and Export Services

Dear Prof. Flannery,

I am writing to congratulate you on your sterling work on AGW climate change.

So what if your dire predictions of Sydney running dry proved groundless, or that the earth has been cooling since 1998, or that the 'hockey stick' evidence was a confidence trick. We now know for certain that Australia's carbon emissions have increased by a scandalous 4% since 1990. And, as you yourself have pointed out, climate change is responsible for the dying out of male circumcision rites in Africa, putting the lives of women at risk from filthy men. I suspect it might also have something to do with the Dry Vagina Syndrome afflicting mature ladies in the developed world.

Keep up the good work.

I was wondering if you would please send me a signed photograph of your good self, and am enclosing $5 to cover postage.

Sincerely,

Mrs. Nancy Singh

Dear Mrs Singh,

Thank you for your letter, though I was distressed to discover that you have been misled as to what I've said about climate change.

Enclosed is a photo, and a copy of my book 'The Weather Makers' which sets the record straight. I hope you enjoy it.

Yours sincerely

Tim [illegible]

3 Sept 08

August 27, 2008

Miss Germaine Greer

NANCY SINGH (MRS)
PO Box 5067
South Murwillimbah
New South Wales 2484
Import and Export Services

Dear Miss Greer,

I am writing to congratulate you on your article on 'Rage'. I agree with every word, although most of the argument is beyond me. I agree that Aborigine men are delinquents and need to be put to work in the coalmines. Hard work, a steady income and women running things at home is what is required. All of this leftwing wringing of hands and sympathy has made matters worse rather than better.

Mr. Singh says that you are the only far-left feminist he has any time for. He remembers you eating oysters with Russell Harty, and often refers to your learned articles on *coitus interruptis.* We are glad to know you are back living in Australia, not far from here. Perhaps we can have tea one day?

I was wondering if you would please send me a signed photograph of your good self for Mr. Singh, and am enclosing $5 to cover postage.

Sincerely,

Mrs. Nancy Singh

August 27, 2008

Mr. Joe Hockey MP

NANCY SINGH (MRS)
PO Box 5067
South Murwillimbah
New South Wales 2484
Import and Export Services

Dear Mr. Hockey,

I wrote to the Speaker, Mr. Harry Jenkins MP a few weeks ago to ask him how Question Time works. I am new to your country and democratic traditions, and at times I find it hard to understand what is going on. I am dismayed that Mr. Jenkins has not replied. I am enclosing a copy of my letter to him. You will see it deals mainly with protocol. I'd welcome some tips from you, if you can spare the time.

I have to say I find big men like yourself captivating, and you come over very well on TV. I was wondering if you would please send me a signed photograph of your good self, and am enclosing $5 to cover postage. (We had better keep this last a little secret from Mr. Singh!).

Sincerely,

Mrs. Nancy Singh

The Hon.

Joe Hockey MP

Member for North Sydney
Shadow Minister for Health and Ageing
Leader of Opposition Business in the House of Representatives

12th September 2008

Mrs Nancy Singh
P O Box 5067
SOUTH MURWILLIMBAH
NSW 2484

Dear Mrs Singh

Thank you for your beautiful letter dated 27th August. I am most humbled and touched by your comments. I would have been happy to cover the cost of postage for the enclosed photograph. As such, I have donated your $5 to a local charity – the Juvenile Diabetes Research Foundation – and enclosed a copy of the receipt for your records.

With respect to the questions addressed to the Speaker, I value your interest. I have attached some fact sheets about the various aspects related to your questions.

Although a Government is responsible for making decisions, they are also responsible to the Parliament and Australia to defend those decisions. One of the more publicly recognisable ways to do this is during Question Time.

Both during Question Time and while the House sits, the Speaker has the role of, in effect, supervising the Parliament. The name Speaker is derived from the fact that the Speaker actually speaks for the House itself by providing direction and advice while the House sits, this is especially so during Question Time.

Question Time is structured to allow the Government, the Opposition and Independent Members of Parliament who are not representatives of a political party, a chance to ask the Government questions.

On average, Question Time runs for an hour and a half each day that Parliament sits with twenty questions being asked – ten by Government Members of the Government and ten by either the Opposition or Independents of the Government.

Question Time provides the Government with time to publicly explain decisions that they have taken. It also provides both the Opposition and Independent Members an opportunity to seek information on issues where the Government is not meeting community expectations.

Level 6, 100 Mount Street, North Sydney **All correspondence to:** PO Box 1107, North Sydney NSW 2059
Telephone (02) 9929 9822 Facsimile (02) 9929 9833 Email: joe@joehockey.com Web: **www.joehockey.com**

Make a Donation

Official Receipt

Transaction Successful

Thank you for your support.

Organisation:	Juvenile Diabetes Research Foundation
Organisation ABN:	40 002 286 553
Organisation Address:	Juvenile Diabetes Research Foundation Level 4, 80 Chandos Street St Leonards, NSW 2065
Donation Date:	Thursday, September 11, 2008 12:57:31 PM
Transaction ID:	1827-3077
Donation Type:	One-off
Donation Amount:	$5.00
Credit Card Number:	4940...891
Expiry Date:	06/2011
Donor Name:	Mr Joe Hockey
Donor Address:	P O Box 1107 North Sydney New South Wales 2059

"My name is Bryce. I have had type 1 diabetes since I was three years old. My one wish would be, 'NO MORE NEEDLES'. Thank you for helping to find a cure."
Bryce Tindall, age 6

For any queries concerning this transaction, please phone Juvenile Diabetes Research Foundation on 03 9696 3866 and quote Transaction ID 1827-3077.

Thank you for your support and generosity.

August 27, 2008

NANCY SINGH (MRS)
PO Box 5067
South Murwillimbah
New South Wales 2484
Import and Export Services

Mr. Harry Jenkins MP
Leader of the House

Dear Mr. Jenkins,

I am disappointed that you have not replied to my letter of 12 July seeking clarity on House protocol. Judging from yesterday's shambles it would seem I am not the only one! I know you are a Very Important Person and have been very busy whilst on holiday these past six weeks, but I thought the Parliament was supposed to represent the people?

Perhaps you are thrifty and were reluctant to incur the costs of posting a photograph to me. If this is the issue, then please find $5 enclosed to cover said expense.

Sincerely,

Mrs. Nancy Singh

SPEAKER'S OFFICE
HOUSE OF REPRESENTATIVES
CANBERRA

8 September 2008

Mrs Nancy Singh
PO Box 5067
South Murwillumbah NSW 2484

Dear Mrs Singh

I refer to your correspondence of 27 August 2008 addressed to the Speaker of the House of Representatives, Harry Jenkins MP. I am responding on behalf of Mr Speaker.

Unfortunately, this office has no record of receiving your correspondence of 12 July 2008. This may be as a consequence of the address used in the more recent letter incorrectly referring to Mr Speaker as "Leader of the House".

Mr Speaker was pleased to sign the enclosed photograph for you and I am returning the $5 note you attached to your letter. Whilst the sentiment is appreciated, cost was not the factor delaying your receipt of the photograph.

Thank you for your interest in the operations of the Parliament.

Yours sincerely

CORA TREVARTHEN
Adviser

August 27, 2008

NANCY SINGH (MRS)
PO Box 5067
South Murwillimbah
New South Wales 2484
Import and Export Services

Miss Jenny Macklin MP
Minister for Families and Aborigines

Dear Miss Macklin,

I am dismayed that you have not bothered to reply to my letter of 8th July. I know of course that you are a Very Important Person, while I am just an ordinary member of society. Also, you have been very busy on a six-week vacation. But I thought public servants were better mannered, as they are in England.

I would only point out that Mr. Noel Pearson and Mr. Anthony Mundine have both said more or less the same as me: that Aborigines need to get jobs if they are ever to make anything of themselves. Left-wing meddling and welfare dependency is so very 1960s, as I am sure you will agree.

Please would you send me a copy of your current policy on Aborigines. I am enclosing $5 to cover postage.

Sincerely,

Mrs. Nancy Singh

Australian Government

Department of Families, Housing, Community Services and Indigenous Affairs

PO Box 7576 Canberra Business Centre ACT 2610
Telephone 1300 653 227
TTY 1800 260 402
www.fahcsia.gov.au

Dear Ms Singh

Please find attached your $5 which we regrettably did not attach to our response to your early letters. We posted our response on 31 October 2008 which you should receive shortly.

Many Thanks
Michael Carruthers

With Compliments

Office of the Hon Jenny Macklin MP
Minister for Families, Housing, Community Services and Indigenous Affairs

Parliament House
CANBERRA ACT 2600

Telephone: *(02) 6277 7560*
Facsimile: *(02) 6273 4122*

MC08-028725

3 1 OCT 2008

Mrs Nancy Singh
PO Box 5067
SOUTH MURWILLIMBAH NSW 2484

Dear Mrs Singh

Thank you for your letters of 8 July and 27 August 2008 to the Minister for Families, Housing, Community Services and Indigenous Affairs, the Hon Jenny Macklin MP, about Indigenous policy. The Minister has asked me to reply on her behalf. I apologise for the lengthy delay in responding.

The Minister appreciates your support and the time you have taken to write to her on these important issues.

You spoke about the need for Indigenous people to be active in the workforce. The Minister agrees that increasing employment opportunities for Indigenous Australians is critical to reducing disadvantage among Aboriginal and Torres Strait Islander people. You may be interested in reading the enclosed paper *Increasing Indigenous Employment Opportunity*, which outlines the Australian Government's preferred model for Indigenous employment programs.

You also asked for a copy of the current policy on Indigenous people. I have enclosed a copy of the Minister's Budget Statement which gives an overview of the Government's policies about Indigenous affairs. It was thoughtful of you to enclose money for postage, however this is not necessary so I am returning it to you.

Thank you again for writing.

Yours sincerely

R Markwell

Ms Rita Markwell
Adviser

Encl.

September 9, 2008

NANCY SINGH (MRS)
PO Box 5067
South Murwillimbah
New South Wales 2484
Import and Export Services

Miss Anna Bligh
Premier
Queensland

Dear Miss Bligh,

Further to my letter of 8th Inst., I am writing to say that I had not taken you for the sort of woman who pockets small sums intended to cover post and packing. I realise that you are a very important person and I am just a member of a hard-working Australian family, but I did expect better from a people's representative.

Sincerely,

Mrs. Nancy Singh

Office of the Premier

Executive Building
100 George Street Brisbane
PO Box 15185 City East
Queensland 4002 Australia
Telephone +61 7 3224 4500
Facsimile +61 7 3221 3631
Email ThePremier@premiers.qld.gov.au
Website www.thepremier.qld.gov.au

22 SEP 2008

Mrs Nancy Singh
PO Box 5067
South Murwillumbah NSW 2484

Dear Mrs Singh

Thank you for your letter received 1 August 2008 regarding offensive slogans on rental camper vans. I have been requested to reply to you on the Premier's behalf.

Your comments regarding the Premier's stance on offensive slogans on rental camper vans have been noted.

As per your request, please find enclosed a signed photograph of the Premier. I also enclose the $5 postage you forwarded. While the Premier appreciates the thought, there is no need for you to pay postage.

Yours sincerely

Nick Williams
Senior Policy Advisor

September 9, 2008

NANCY SINGH (MRS)
PO Box 5067
South Murwillimbah
New South Wales 2484
Import and Export Services

Mr. David Cameron MP
Leader of the Conservative Party

Dear Mr. Cameron,

I read recently that you are considering introducing Sharia Law for the theft of bicycles. Whilst I agree that street crime is out of control in Brown's Britain – all those black youths knifing each other in broad daylight – I would urge you not to meddle with the Muslim menace. Sadly, violence and intolerance is a way of life for the Islamists, and one that is out of step with dear old Blighty. Sharia law would only encourage more barbarism.

As you can see, Mr. Singh and I now live in Australia. We left Britain to get away from Tony Blair, stealth taxes and the politically correct far left. Sadly, in Kevin Rudd, we now have a poor man's Tony Blair who is completely out of his depth. The country is going downhill fast.

We are hoping for a Conservative victory at the next election. I hope you will return Britain to civility and decency, and get rid of the Equalities Commission and Trevor Phillips.

I hope this advice is helpful to you. I am enclosing $5 to cover postage as I should be most grateful if you would send me a signed photo of your charming self.

Sincerely,

Mrs. Nancy Singh

Mrs Nancy Singh
PO Box 5067
Murwillimbah
New South Wales 2484
Australia

Wednesday, 17th September 2008

Dear Mrs Singh,

I am writing on behalf of David Cameron to thank you for your letter of 9th September 2008.

We are grateful to you for taking the time and trouble to get in touch, and we certainly do take on board the points you make in your letter. I will certainly pass on your views to David.

As requested, I enclose a signed p photograph of David for your collection and return your $5 bill with this reply.

Thank you again for writing.

Yours sincerely,

Ian Pendlington
Office of the Leader of the Opposition

Conservative Campaign Headquarters, 30 Millbank, London SW1P 4DP, Switchboard

September 9, 2008

Director of TV Entertainment
ABC

NANCY SINGH (MRS)
PO Box 5067
South Murwillimbah
New South Wales 2484
Import and Export Services

INVOICE

To the supply of humorous material:

$1000 only.

Sincerely,

Mrs. Nancy Singh

September 9, 2008

Director
Channel 9 TV

NANCY SINGH (MRS)
PO Box 5067
South Murwillimbah
New South Wales 2484
Import and Export Services

Dear Sir,

I am writing to draw your attention to a quite shocking lapse of decency during a recent broadcast. In the middle of your coverage of the Ladies Final at the US Tennis Open, one of your commentators made a remark that 'Serena is barely breaking wind.' I have no idea how he would know this?

I am wondering if you would confirm that this remark was indeed broadcast as I have difficulty believing that you would have allowed this to air. It was during the second game of the second set.

Many thanks for your help.

Sincerely,

Mrs. Nancy Singh

November 7, 2008

Mrs Nancy Singh
PO Box 5067
South Murwillimbah
NSW 2484

Dear Nancy,

I am in receipt of your letter dated September 9 regarding a line of commentary used during Nine's US Open tennis coverage.

It was an unfortunate turn of phrase. There was no offence intended.

Yours sincerely,

Lesley Tapsall
Executive Producer
Wide World of Sports

NINE NETWORK AUSTRALIA PTY LTD

Postal Address: PO Box 27 Willoughby NSW 2068 Street Address: 24 Artarmon Road Willoughby NSW 2068 Australia

PH: 61 2 9965 2625 ninemsn.com.au FAX 61 2 9437 6534 ABN 88 008 685 407

September 9, 2008

Prof. Tim Flannery,

NANCY SINGH (MRS)
PO Box 5067
South Murwillimbah
New South Wales 2484
Import and Export Services

Dear Prof. Flannery,

Thank you so much for your letter of 4th Inst. and for sending me a copy of your book *The Weather Makers*. This is very kind of you. I shall read it carefully to see if I can understand the theory of AGW which, I freely admit, so far I find about as scientific as astrology or Marxism.

With all good wishes,

Sincerely,

Mrs. Nancy Singh

September 9, 2008

The Gold Coast Rotary Club

NANCY SINGH (MRS)
PO Box 5067
South Murwillimbah
New South Wales 2484
Import and Export Services

Dear Sir,

I am writing in response to your item on brassieres and Third World women in the *Tweed Sun.*

I had no idea the situation was so grave, that such women are prone to 'rashes, fungal infections and abscesses … between the breasts'. It is certainly humbling to think that second-hand bras are 'especially welcome because they normally don't attract import duty'. Who would have thought that 'worn-out bras can be used for spare parts'?

I am surprised that the larger sizes are the hardest to get, as I rather thought most Third World women would be small. I myself am only as 32B, just right according to Mr. Singh.

Would you accept such a small bra, and where should I post it to?

Sincerely,

Mrs. Nancy Singh

September 9, 2008

NANCY SINGH (MRS)
PO Box 5067
South Murwillimbah
New South Wales 2484
Import and Export Services

Mr. Trevor Phillips
Chairman
Equalities Commission

Dear Mr. Phillips,

A well-meaning member of your admin staff responded to my letter of 9th inst. Her letter was badly written, and I can see that you too have problems finding basically educated staff under a Labour government.

My main purpose in writing to you was to ask how you intend to make Britain less 'hideously white'? I'd be grateful if you would send me a copy of your policy on this matter.

It is a pity you 'don't do' signed photographs as I had always considered you an attractive and friendly-looking man.

Sincerely,

Mrs. Nancy Singh

Equality and
Human Rights
Commission

equalityhumanrights.com

Mrs Nancy Singh
PO Box 5067
Murwillimbah
New South Wales 2484

Our ref: TP/KG/239Singh
Date: 19 September 2008

Thank you for your letter of 9 September to Trevor Phillips, who has asked me to respond on his behalf.

I am sorry – and surprised - that you felt my previous letter to you was badly written. As you will appreciate, Mr Phillips receives many letters and he is not able to reply to them all personally.

You asked how Mr Phillips intends to make Britain less 'hideously white'. I should say first of all that when he used this phrase he was quoting former BBC Director-General Greg Dyke, who made the comment in the context of expressing concerns about the representation of ethnic minorities in the media. Mr Phillips recently made a speech on that theme which outlines his policy, and I have enclosed a copy of it for your information.

I trust that this addresses your query.

Yours sincerely

Karen Grayson
Policy Adviser to the Chair

Equality and
Human Rights
Commission

3 More London Riverside
Tooley Street
London SE1 2RG

Tel: 0203 117 0235
Fax: 020 7407 7557
info@equalityhumanrights.com

The Equality and Human Rights Commission was established by the Equality Act 2006 as the Commission for Equality and Human Rights.

September 9, 2008

Mr. Lindsay Tanner
Minister for Finance

NANCY SINGH (MRS)
PO Box 5067
South Murwillimbah
New South Wales 2484
Import and Export Services

Dear Mr. Tanner,

Thank you for your letter, it is good of you to write. I am sorry if I have misunderstood your position, or indeed have expressed myself clumsily.

Of course, I accept your word that the government is not trying to engineer a recession. It is just that we are coming perilously close to one, just as in the USA, Europe and the UK. In my humble opinion this is all the fault of the Federal Reserves who should have left things as they were instead of mucking about with interest rate hikes. On this, I cannot see that putting inflation up to over 5% (largely by increasing mortgage costs, bank charges and rents) is a 'successful outcome', neither is unemployment at 5%.

I read your blog on the luxury car tax the other day. I am afraid it was not very convincing as you will have gathered from the comments posted in reply. The first rule of economics is to reduce taxation wherever and whenever possible. The luxury car tax is not worth a candle; it reminds me of the window tax in 18th century Bath – all greed and no light.

Mr. Singh and I left the UK to get away from Tony Blair, rampant street crime, Muslim fanatics and 'stealth taxes'. Mr. Singh says Labour governments always make a mess of the economy. I just thought it would take a little longer than 9 months.

Sincerely,

Mrs. Nancy Singh

NO RESPONSE

September 9, 2008

NANCY SINGH (MRS)
PO Box 5067
South Murwillimbah
New South Wales 2484
Import and Export Services

Miss Margaret Throsby
Classic FM
ABC Radio

Dear Miss Throsby,

I am writing to ask if you would possibly mind having fewer left-wing moaners and psycho-babblers on your show. Mr. Singh and I like to tune in for classical music, not to hear a load of biased politically correct nonsense.

The proper place for this sort of thing is surely on Radio National along with Phillip Adams and all the other Marxists. It is striking that you never have proper people on, such as Arthur Herman or that amazing Somalian woman who renounced Islam – both were in Sydney recently.

I realise of course that the ABC is a hotbed of far left activists, but you could at least pretend to be balanced from time to time.

Sincerely,

Mrs. Nancy Singh

September 9, 2008

Miss Oprah Winfrey

NANCY SINGH (MRS)
PO Box 5067
South Murwillimbah
New South Wales 2484
Import and Export Services

Dear Miss Winfrey,

I am writing to say that Mr. Singh and I and many others are saddened at your decision to ban Mrs. Sarah Palin from your program. She is just the sort of person we are interested in, balancing as she does a family life, political career and the everyday considerations of being a woman. She is very bright and attractive, and has views on many issues with which we agree too. I suppose you are upset at her for not being black.

We usually watch your program, even although these days your guests are mostly lefties. Personally I prefer Dr. Phil. I think it is a mistake for you to become involved in politics.

I am wondering if you would be so good as to send me a photo of your good self with Mr. John McCain? I am enclosing $5 to cover the postage.

Sincerely,

Mrs. Nancy Singh

September 12, 2008

Mr. Chris Bowen MP
Minister for Grocery Prices

NANCY SINGH (MRS)
PO Box 5067
South Murwillimbah
New South Wales 2484
Import and Export Services

Dear Mr. Bowen,

I am disappointed not to have received a reply from you to my letter of 14th Inst. I know you are a Very Important Person and I am only a common worker, but I am in fact an Australian citizen and thought public servants would reply to letters from the electorate.

I take it you do not agree with my proposal for a *WineWatch* scheme to complement and extend your own *GroceryWatch* and *FuelWatch*, and the proposed *BankWatch*. There is also, I seem to recall, a proposal for a *ChildcareWatch*.

I am strongly of the view that the less governments meddle with things they don't understand, the better; yet I am not sure that watching things is much about anything either? It all smacks a bit of *1984*.

It is reassuring that despite the 'education crisis', the 'climate change challenge', the 'skills crisis', 'the housing affordability crisis', the 'inflation genie', 'hard-working Australian families doing it tough', the 'productivity crisis' and so, the government is content to watch.

Sincerely,

Mrs. Nancy Singh

September 12, 2008

Mr. Kevin Foley
Deputy Premier, South Australia

NANCY SINGH (MRS)
PO Box 5067
South Murwillimbah
New South Wales 2484
Import and Export Services

Dear Mr. Foley,

We don't get much news about Adelaide here on the Gold Coast, but we did hear all about your gaffe in dismissing the Commonwealth Games as a second rate event. I agree with your subsequent admission that this was a very stupid thing to say.

Nevertheless it is clear that Adelaide needs to attract visitors and spending to help boost a slow economy, and to overcome its image as Australia's capital for bizarre murders. Here are what I hope are a couple of helpful suggestions:

1. Given Adelaide's older population profile, why not host the world championship carpet bowls tournament?

2. Or an event on how to write books that only the over 60s read? Unless the Writers' Festival does this already. I can't imagine who else reads Germaine Greer these days.

3. Perhaps you could get Prof. Tim Flannery to give his learned lecture on global warming and its impact on male circumcision in Africa?

I am sure if you put your mind to it there are no shortage of circuses one could stage. I understand that Mr. Rann is in line to be the next Australian Ambassador to Italy, so you may be the new Premier very soon. It is important to show initiative and that you are your own man. I hope these small suggestions help.

Sincerely,

Mrs. Nancy Singh

Government
of South Australia

Office of the
Deputy Premier
Treasurer
Minister for Industry and Trade
Minister for Federal/State Relations

TRS08D1422

23 September 2008

Mrs Nancy Singh
PO Box 5067
SOUTH MURWILLIMBAH NSW 2484

Dear Mrs Singh

I write on behalf of the Deputy Premier to acknowledge receipt of your letter dated 12 September.

Your correspondence has been drawn to the Minister's attention.

Yours sincerely

Meredith Dobbin
SENIOR ADMINISTRATIVE OFFICER

State Administration Centre • 200 Victoria Square • Adelaide SA 5000 • GPO Box 2264 • Adelaide SA 5001 • DX 56203
T: (08) 8226 1866 • F: (08) 8226 1896 • E: treasurer@saugov.sa.gov.au

September 12, 2008

Mrs. Harriet Harman MP

NANCY SINGH (MRS)
PO Box 5067
South Murwillimbah
New South Wales 2484
Import and Export Services

Dear Mrs. Harman,

I am disappointed not to have received a reply from you to my letter of 9th Inst. I know you are a Very Important Person and I am only a common worker, but I am in fact a British citizen and thought public servants would reply to letters from the electorate. I am also surprised that you are the sort who would pocket $5 meant for postage.

I see that you are now calling for a new class war and further tax attacks on the wealthy. When will you socialists ever learn that such measures are counter-productive, and simply drive the wealthy away, taking their taxes, investments and job creation with them? If it weren't for the wealthy and the aspiring middle classes, there would be no public schools to which you could send your own children.

Sincerely,

Mrs. Nancy Singh

RT. HON. HARRIET HARMAN Q.C. M.P.

CM

HOUSE OF COMMONS
LONDON SW1A 0AA
Tel: 020 7219 4218
Fax: 020 7219 4877
Email: harmanh@parliament.uk
www.harrietharman.labour.co.uk

Nancy Singh
PO Box 5067
South Murwillimbah
New South Wales
2484
Australia

26th September 2008

Dear Nancy,

Thank you for your letters dated 9th August and 12th September 2008, please accept my apologies for the delayed response.

I am proud to have represented in Parliament the constituency of Camberwell and Peckham for the past 25 years. I am in the constituency holding advice surgeries, knocking on doors and attending local events on a regular basis without any security equipment.

On 31st March 2008 I went on a visit with the local police to highlight the important work they do.

The wearing of protective equipment is mandatory for officers when on patrol and as such the Police deemed it appropriate that anyone who accompanies them on their duties wears a Met Vest as well. This includes representatives from the local communities, MPs or members of the media. I put on a jacket they offered me without questioning it.

I have worked hard over the years to increase the numbers of Police in Camberwell and Peckham. Increased police numbers is one of the top demands my constituents have made over the years. 1000 is the number of officers Southwark Police said they need to carry out their duties. In response, I launched the 'Police 1000' campaign in 2002, which aims to raise the number of police officers in Southwark to 1000.

On top of the 873 police officer posts and 87 PCSO posts allocated to Southwark, there are currently 30 of the Metropolitan Special Constabulary posted to Southwark with significant growth anticipated in the future. In addition, there are 19 members of the Met volunteers Programme and 25 volunteer police cadets. Southwark Police are also in negotiation with the local authority to fund an additional 22 PCSO posts.

Since I launched the campaign in 2002 we have gained 98 police officers, but I remain committed to getting the 40 more needed to achieve 1000 police officers in Southwark.

RT. HON. HARRIET HARMAN Q.C. M.P.

HOUSE OF COMMONS

LONDON SW1A 0AA

Tel: 020 7219 4218
Fax: 020 7219 4877
Email: harmanh@parliament.uk
www.harrietharman.labour.co.uk

I will continue to work along side Southwark Police and support the good work that they do. The Neighbourhood Policing Teams which have been operating in Southwark for the past two years have now been introduced to every neighbourhood in the UK. Since they were introduced in Peckham Ward, where I patrolled on 31st March 2008, crime has dropped by 20%. People like to know the name and phone number of their local Officers.

Best Wishes,

Harriet Harman QC MP

September 12, 2008

Mr. Boris Johnson
Lord Mayor of London

NANCY SINGH (MRS)
PO Box 5067
South Murwillimbah
New South Wales 2484
Import and Export Services

Dear Mr. Johnson

I am disappointed not to have received a reply from you to my letter of 12th Inst. I know you are a Very Important Person and I am only a common worker, but I am in fact a British citizen and thought public servants would reply to letters from the electorate.

I also understand that you have been very busy going on holiday and swanning about in China, but I was taught that everyday decencies are all important. I certainly never took you for the type of cove who would pocket $5 meant for postage!

I do hope that easy charm you exude is not a sham. We need you to see off New Labour, who have ruined Britain and turned it over to violent gangs, black gangsta culture and mad Muslim murderers. I suppose it is too late to exile the Islamists?

Sincerely,

Mrs. Nancy Singh

September 12, 2008

NANCY SINGH (MRS)
PO Box 5067
South Murwillimbah
New South Wales 2484
Import and Export Services

Monsieur Nicolai Sarkozy
President de France
Paris
France

Dear Monsieur Sarkozy,

J'ecrit pour dit que vous etes l'homme plus de bon chance du monde. Votre femme, elle est tres, tres belle. Et aussi tres artistique. Je pense que Tony Blair et tous les autres sont verte avec l'envy!.

J'espere que vous voulez moi donner une photographe de vous et votre femme, avec Mr. Bush ou Queen Elizabeth? Je m'enclose $5 pour la postage. Merci beaucoups.

Vive La France!

Sincerely,

Mrs. Nancy Singh

Le Chef de Cabinet
du Président de la République

Madame Nancy SINGH
PO Box 5067
South Murwillimbah
NEW SOUTH WALES 2484
AUSTRALIE

Paris, le - 6 OCT. 2008

Chère Madame,

Le Président de la République française a bien reçu votre lettre.

Sensible à votre aimable démarche, Monsieur Nicolas SARKOZY m'a confié le soin de vous en remercier.

Je dois néanmoins vous préciser qu'il n'existe pas de photographie officielle du couple présidentiel.

Par ailleurs, il m'est agréable de joindre à ce courrier, comme vous l'avez demandé, le portrait officiel dédicacé du Chef de l'Etat.

Je vous prie d'agréer, Chère Madame, l'expression de mes sentiments les meilleurs.

Cédric GOUBET

Référence à rapp
SCP/UT/B13998

September 12, 2008

NANCY SINGH (MRS)
PO Box 5067
South Murwillimbah
New South Wales 2484
Import and Export Services

Mr. Glenn Stevens,
Governor of the Federal Reserve Bank

Dear Mr. Stevens,

Thank you so much for your letter of 13th August. I am grateful to you, and know this must be a busy and anxious time for you. I accept your word that Messrs Greenspan and Bernanke are not imbeciles, but I still believe they panicked into raising rates far too soon, and so have caused not only the downturn but also triggered the credit shortage.

As for inflation, I have seen no compelling evidence that Australia was severely overheating in 2006 and 2007. The price rises of that time were caused by Cyclone Larry (bananas), the drought (wheat, milk, fruit and veg), followed by oil prices and the resultant knock-on costs. Putting up interest rates had no impact at all on oil prices, or food for that matter. But they did add to price increases in mortgages, rent and bank fees, charges and overdrafts. Because of this, inflation is heading towards 5%.

I know I am just a silly woman, but I cannot help feel that riding out the food price surge would have been a better policy. Customers begin to reduce spending of their own volition, or shop elsewhere, or indeed buy less. Falling volumes of demand then produce price cuts. I now shop at Aldi for tinned produce and I get my veggies from farms and roadside stalls. I have noticed some prices coming down in the supermarkets, though not petrol.

I wonder if there is a theory of inflation that seeks to draw a distinction between actual inflation (decline in the value of money) as opposed to price increases during an up-cycle, which must surely be part and parcel of wealth creation? I seem to recall of Prof. Okun in the 1970s who proposed a 'Discomfort Index' on perfectly sensible grounds that putting up unemployment to lower inflation only makes matters worse. I think I have an old article on this somewhere.

Wishing you success in achieving a soft landing.

Sincerely,
Mrs. Nancy Singh

NANCY SINGH (MRS)
PO Box 5067
South Murwillimbah
New South Wales 2484
Import and Export Services

September 14, 2008

Director General
BBC
Bush House
London

Dear Sir,

We don't really pay much attention to dreary old Britain these days, having left to get away from Tony Blair, high taxes, political correctness and the moaning, left-wing bias of the BBC. We don't even watch your World News as the voices of your presenters are depressing. However, we did see that you commissioned a 'poll' of British voters and their preferred US President.

Is this not somewhat presumptuous? Why should the Americans pay any attention to yet another rigged survey, whether by the BBC or the *Guardian*? It is also a waste of licence fee payers' money. I am glad we don't have a licence fee – and the Big Brother snooping you stoop to – here in Australia. The ABC here, of course, wishes to follow your example and spend millions on unnecessary digital channels that no-one watches. The BBC really should be pared back to Radios 3 and 4, BBC 2 and the World Service (radio, not TV). I hope the Conservatives will attend to this as a matter of urgency.

The only thing we miss about the BBC is Jeremy Paxman, about the only heterosexual white man you have left, unless you count the Welsh windbag Humphries. Would you please send me a photo of Mr. Paxman. I am enclosing $5 to cover the postage.

Sincerely,

Mrs. Nancy Singh

British Broadcasting Corporation PO Box 1922 Glasgow G2 3WT Telephone 03700 100 222

BBC Information

Mrs Nancy Singh
Po Box 5067
South Murwillimbah
New South Wales
2484

Our Ref 15879139

13 October 2008

Dear Mrs Singh

Thank you for your letter of September 14 addressed to the Director General regarding receiving a signed photgraph of Jeremy Paxman.

As I am sure you will appreciate, the Director General receives more correspondence than he can deal with personally, so once letters have been read they are forwarded by his office to BBC Information. This department has a wealth of knowledge about BBC programmes and policies and is experienced in the workings of the Corporation. The Director General has therefore authorised us to reply on his behalf.

I understand you would like a signed photgraph of Jeremy, as you think he is the best presenter on the BBC.

BBC personalities or their agents are responsible for handling their own correspondence, but we will be more than happy to forward letters on via our Artists' Mail department. In order to do this, however, letters must be addressed to each artist individually, individually stamped and addressed to:

(Name of Celebrity)
(Name of Programme)
Artists' Mail
BBC TV Centre
Wood Lane
London
W12 7RJ

Please replace the information in brackets and write 'Private and Personal - Please Forward' at the top of each envelope. You must write to each artist individually or we are unable to pass the letters on.

Please also find enclosed your five dollars

Thank you again for your interest in the BBC and for taking the trouble to write.

Yours sincerely

David Shields
BBC Information

Encs

September 14, 2008

NANCY SINGH (MRS)
PO Box 5067
South Murwillimbah
New South Wales 2484
Import and Export Services

Mr. Al Gore
Ex Vice-President of the United States of America

Dear Mr. Gore,

I am writing to ask your advice on a sensitive matter of conscience. Mr. Singh and I are committed to saving the planet as much as the next person. We like to buy a new car every two years to keep abreast of technological developments and fuel-efficient engines. Normally we buy a Mercedes, an Audi or a BMW but this year these cars are facing a hike in so-called 'luxury car tax' here in Australia.

I am wondering if you know which models are currently the best for the environment, perhaps the very car that you yourself drive? Any advice would be much appreciated.

While we are on the subject of carbon finger-printing, Mr. Singh and I also own several houses and investment properties. We are concerned that perhaps we have too many for the good of the planet. How many houses do you think it is proper for a married couple to own?

I was hoping you would please send me a signed photograph of your good self, and am enclosing $5 to cover postage.

Sincerely,

Mrs. Nancy Singh

Al Gore

September 16, 2008

NANCY SINGH (MRS)
PO Box 5067
South Murwillimbah
New South Wales 2484
Import and Export Services

Director General
Sky News

Dear Sir,

I have just been watching your coverage of the Liberal Party leadership election. Wasn't it exciting!? Great coverage, thank you.

I was wondering if you have any vacancies going as a correspondent covering Parliament? I realise that there is stiff competition for such places, and I am sadly no longer as young and bonny as I once was, but I would lend an air of maturity. I am not on the far left of politics either, as in the case of Mr. David Spiers, but I suppose I could learn to toe the line and to support Mr. Rudd in every eventuality.

Please would you send me a job application form. I am enclosing $5 to cover the postage.

Sincerely,

Mrs. Nancy Singh

September 16, 2008

NANCY SINGH (MRS)
PO Box 5067
South Murwillimbah
New South Wales 2484
Import and Export Services

Mr. John Murphy MP
Parliamentary Secretary
Canberra
ACT

Dear Mr. Murphy,

I am sorry to learn of your difficulties with the new caterers in Parliament House. I can see how frustrating it is for you and your colleagues to be served food in portions that are too small or that has not even been microwaved to the correct temperature. The humiliating treatment meted out to your wife over the now infamous 'Beef Stroganoff' incident is most distressing. Beef Stroganoff is also a favourite of mine and of the ladies with whom I lunch.

It is a shame you will probably be unable to get rid of the staff in question as most likely they have one of Miss Gillard's new workplace agreements.

Please would you pass on my good wishes to your wife.

Sincerely,

Mrs. Nancy Singh

September 16, 2008

NANCY SINGH (MRS)
PO Box 5067
South Murwillimbah
New South Wales 2484
Import and Export Services

Miss Alison Turner
Public Services Coordinator
Greater London Authority

Dear Miss Turner,

Thank you for your letter of 5th Inst. At first I could not recall having written to you, until I realised you are replying on behalf of Mr. Boris Johnson. Is he as gorgeous in the flesh as on TV?

I am only writing back to explain that I sent a second letter to Mr. Johnson and to advise you just to ignore this.

I am slightly puzzled at your comments on 'challenging discrimination', as I had written to express support for Mr. Johnson. More broadly, it is my view that Britain needs to discriminate a lot more in terms of decency, manners, morality and facing up to the fact that too many jihadists are plotting to kill us from within the country. I am a believer in live and let live, providing loud-mouthed special interest groups – left-wing teachers, radical Muslims, gay rights activists and infantile greenies – do the same.

Sincerely,

Mrs. Nancy Singh

September 18, 2008

NANCY SINGH (MRS)
PO Box 5067
South Murwillimbah
New South Wales 2484
Import and Export Services

Miss Julia Gillard MP
Minister for Productivity, Education and Socialism

Dear Miss Gillard,

I am dismayed that you have not bothered to reply to my letter of 14th August. I know of course that you are a Very Important Person, while I am just an ordinary 'hard-working Australian family member'. Also, you have been very busy on a six-week vacation. But I thought public servants were better mannered, as they are in England. Also, I had not thought of you as the sort of person who would pocket $5 intended for postage.

Another example of the basic lack of manners in Australian public life is Question Time in Parliament, a quite disgraceful spectacle of evasion, spin and false accusations. You might as well cancel it altogether. I notice you accused Mr. Malcolm Turnbull of being a leading proponent of 'Work Choices'. Strange, but I seem to think it was Mrs. Rudd's company who had workers on the dreaded Australian Workplace Agreements and was paying below the minimum wage. Perhaps this has slipped your mind.

Please would you send me a copy of your new policy on workplace relations. Please feel free to use the $5 I sent you to cover the postage, so as to save 'blowing a hole' in the surplus.

Sincerely,

Mrs. Nancy Singh

Australian Government

Department of Education, Employment and Workplace Relations

Your Ref
Our Ref MC08-030985

Ms Nancy Singh
PO Box 5067
SOUTH MURWILLIMBAH NSW 2484

Dear Ms Singh

Thank you for your letter of 18 September 2008 to the Hon Julia Gillard MP, Minister for Employment and Workplace Relations, concerning the workplace relations policy of the Australian Government. The Minister has asked me to reply on her behalf.

Please note, there is no record of you correspondence of 14 August 2008 as being received.

The workplace relations policy of the Australian Government is to remove Work Choices (the workplace relations system of the previous Government) and to create a fairer and simpler system that achieves the right balance between employers and employees. To give employers and employees the time they need to work through the transition to the new system without disruption or confusion, the Australian Government is undertaking a measured and consultative approach to its introduction.

As a first step, the Australian Government introduced into Parliament the *Workplace Relations Amendment (Transition to Forward with Fairness) Act 2008.* This Act, which came into effect on 28 March 2008, prevents any more individual Australian Workplace Agreements being made.

The next step to be taken in the removal of Work Choices will come at the end of this year when the Australian Government introduces its substantive workplace relations legislation into Parliament.

The substantive legislation will involve putting in place a new workplace relations system to replace Work Choices built on:

- a strong safety net of 10 legislated National Employment Standards for all employees
- a modern, simple award system that complements the National Employment Standards, providing certainty, flexibility and stability for employers and their employees
- an enterprise-level collective bargaining system focussed on promoting productivity

16–18 Mort Street, Canberra ACT 2601
GPO Box 9880, Canberra ACT 2601 | Phone (02) 6121 6000
www.deewr.gov.au | ABN 63 578 775 294

- unfair dismissal laws which balance the rights of employees to be protected from unfair dismissal with the need for employers, particularly small business, to fairly and efficiently manage their workforce

- a 'one-stop shop', Fair Work Australia, to ensure fair treatment at work by providing advice and support on all workplace relations issues and enforcement of legal entitlements.

The Australian Government is committed to the new system being fully operational by 1 January 2010 but it also intends to commence key elements, including the bargaining framework, the unfair dismissal provisions and the associated protections, on 1 July 2009 following Parliamentary approval of the substantive legislation.

If you are interested in following developments in the removal of Work Choices and its replacement by a new workplace relations system, you may wish to refer to the relevant website at the Department of Education, Employment and Workplace Relations, www.workplace.gov.au. I have also included some documents which more fully outline the Australian Government's workplace relations policies.

Thank you for bringing your concerns to the attention of the Australian Government.

Yours sincerely

Stewart Thomas
Branch Manager
Strategic Coordination Branch
Workplace Relations Policy Group

31 October 2008

September 18, 2008

Mrs. Belinda Neal MP

NANCY SINGH (MRS)
PO Box 5067
South Murwillimbah
New South Wales 2484
Import and Export Services

Dear Mrs. Neal,

I am a little disappointed that you have not replied to my letter of 8th July, although I understand that you have been fighting criminal charges.

You are one of the few politicians I feel is trustworthy, and one can see the goodness shining out of your face. I was wondering if you would send me a photo of your good self. I am enclosing $5 to cover postage.

Sincerely,

Mrs. Nancy Singh

September 21, 2008

Emma Ayres
Classic FM
ABC

NANCY SINGH (MRS)
PO Box 5067
South Murwillimbah
New South Wales 2484
Import and Export Services

Dear Emma,

I am so pleased that you have taken my advice and gotten rid of Margaret Throsby and all her dreadful left-wing moaning. The morning programming is now so much better, and I especially like the poetry and other recitations. I like your voice better too.

Many thanks,

Sincerely,

Mrs. Nancy Singh

September 21, 2008

NANCY SINGH (MRS)
PO Box 5067
South Murwillimbah
New South Wales 2484
Import and Export Services

The Producer
The View

Dear Sir or Madam,

I am writing to say how offensive I found the women's behaviour during the recent guest appearance by Cindy and John McCain. Why were they so rude and aggressive towards the Senator and his wife?

The fat Jewish one was particularly hostile in her questioning. The real give-away, however, was the body language of Barbara Walters towards Mr. McCain. One might be forgiven for imagining that the Senator had been rolling about in the *ordure*, possibly with a pig. I am surprised you encourage this sort of thing on national television. It makes the US media look very bad around the world.

I have decided that I shall no longer be watching *The View*, or *Oprah* for that matter, as I am more than a little tired of C-listers using airtime to propagate left-wing bias. I am wondering if you would be so good as to send me a photo of Mr. and Mrs. John McCain? I am enclosing $5 to cover the postage.

Sincerely,

Mrs. Nancy Singh

September 21, 2008

Mr. Kevin Rude MP
Prime Minister

NANCY SINGH (MRS)
PO Box 5067
South Murwillimbah
New South Wales 2484
Import and Export Services

Dear Mr. Rudd,

I am disappointed that you have now failed to reply to two letters. I can see that during your hard upbringing in the back of a Ford Falcon that your mother had no time to teach you manners or decent behaviour. This may explain why you turn your back on people in Parliament. You may be as wealthy as Mr. Malcolm Turnbull but you lack his poise and good breeding.

Since you have raised the question of how much wealth Mr. Turnbull has accumulated due to his own hard work, I should like – for reasons of comparative research – to know how much money you have made from your wife's companies, including those that paid below the minimum wage.

Also, would you be able to confirm that Mr. Mike Rann's reward for acting as attack dog is the next Ambassadorship to Italy where, I understand, he has developed a taste for truffles.

Sincerely,

Mrs. Nancy Singh

September 22, 2008

NANCY SINGH (MRS)
PO Box 5067
South Murwillimbah
New South Wales 2484
Import and Export Services

Mr. A. C. McAndrew,
Pro Vice Cancellor
Griffith University

Dear Mr. McAndrew,

I thank you for your letter of 23 July, unsigned. I note that you are happy to take money from Muslims but not Hindus.

I am afraid I could not understand a word of the second paragraph. I assume this is the latest in trendy post-modern 'blame whitey' gobbledegook. What, pray tell, is 'a balanced and contextualised understanding of Islam'? Does it include flying planes into buildings? Or the East African slave trade? Or the various wars and terrorist campaigns in Indonesia, the Middle East, Russia, Serbia, China and Iran? Do you think it is a good thing for Iran to have nuclear weapons?

I have recently been reading a copy of the *Griffith Review.* I am surprised at its obvious and extreme bias towards Marxism. If this is indicative of the sort of ship you run, then I suspect it will not be long before sensible people send their children elsewhere. Perhaps you should open a new Griffith Research Centre for Leftwing Studies? I am sure George Soros and other fifth columnists would contribute.

Sincerely,

Mrs. Nancy Singh

September 22, 2008

Miss Nicola Roxon MP
Minister for Health

NANCY SINGH (MRS)
PO Box 5067
South Murwillimbah
New South Wales 2484
Import and Export Services

Dear Miss Roxon,

A very kind member of your admin team, Virginia Hart, has written to me explaining your 'National Binge Drinking Strategy'. I am afraid I don't find it very convincing. I wonder, for example, why you have picked out sports organisations for special treatment when everyone knows that the worst drunks are artists, writers and luvvies. Maybe the arts should be banned from accepting sponsorship from the demon drink. One can see it all ending up like Sweden where everyone is dour and morose.

Miss Hart also notes that your government is about to release a 'National Preventative Health Strategy', including 'facing the obesity challenge' as Mr. Rudd would say. I find it surprising that you are so keen on all these 'National' strategies on infrastructure, education and health, as this is the very sort of language that despots used in the last century. The words national and socialism do not look well in the same sentence.

My latest idea is to have a high profile advertising campaign to tackle obesity. This would involve several high-profile Members going on a sponsored diet. Candidates might include Jenny Macklin and Mrs. Rudd, Belinda Neal and John Murphy's wife. It is a pity that Julie Bishop is so trim, but maybe Joe Hockey would participate, although he looks very handsome as he is.

I think this would be a great contribution to reducing obesity, and look forward to your reply.

Sincerely,

Mrs. Nancy Singh

Australian Government

Department of Health and Ageing

Mrs N Singh
PO Box 5067
SOUTH MURWILLIMBAH NSW 2484

Dear Mrs Singh

I am writing to acknowledge receipt of your letter of 22 September 2008 to the Minister for Health and Ageing, the Hon Nicola Roxon MP.

Minister Roxon has forwarded your correspondence to the Department for further attention.

Yours sincerely

JM Connor
Ministerial Liaison and Support Section
1 October 2008

Portfolio Strategies Division MDP 41 GPO Box 9848 Canberra ACT 2601
Telephone: (02) 6289 1555 Fax: (02) 6289 1250 ABN 83 605 426 759

October 5, 2008

NANCY SINGH (MRS)
PO Box 5067
South Murwillimbah
New South Wales 2484
Import and Export Services

Miss Karen Middleton
SBS Television

Dear Miss Middleton,

I have just been watching *Insiders* on the ABC. I think it is good that they allow someone with such trenchant left-wing views to appear on the show.

This has prompted me to write to you to ask if you would be willing to join a campaign to reduce obesity in Australia. My idea is that prominent left-wing women, such as Mrs. Rudd, Miss Macklin and Miss Roxon should participate in a sponsored weight-loss program to demonstrate the benefits of eating less and taking exercise from time to time. I have already written to the Health Minister asking for support.

I am sure you will see how important it is for young people and others to have role models who live healthy lifestyles. To help with this I should like to take before and after shots of participating individuals. I wonder if you could send me a current picture of your good self. I am enclosing $5 to cover postage.

Keep up the good work on the ABC!

Sincerely,

Mrs. Nancy Singh

October 11, 2008

NANCY SINGH (MRS)
PO Box 5067
South Murwillimbah
New South Wales 2484
Import and Export Services

Mr. Gordon Brown MP
Prime Minister of the United Kingdom

Dear Mr. Brown,

I am sorry to see that you have not followed my advice and sacked half your Cabinet. I suppose keeping Darling on is a good move so he can take the blame for the banking collapse. This follows in the long line of Scots mucking up the financial system as in the case of the Ayr Bank collapse of 1772, and John Laws and the Mississippi Bubble. The great Adam Smith had nothing but scorn for do-good banks such as Fannie Mae.

But bringing Peter Mandelson back is sheer folly. I don't know what has possessed you. I wouldn't trust Mandelson as far as I could throw him. He is venal, and so bright that he gave himself kidney stones by drinking dodgy Chinese milk! Mind you, he does have personal experience of mortgage fraud. He is also a homosexual. As the old saying goes, 'He who sups with the devil should keep his back to the wall'.

I was wondering if you would send me a photo of your good self and your bonnie wife. I am enclosing $5 to cover the postage.

Sincerely,

Mrs. Nancy Singh

10 DOWNING STREET
LONDON SW1A 2AA
www.number10.gov.uk

From the Direct Communications Unit 21 October 2008

Mrs Nancy Singh
PO Box 5067
South Murwillimbah
New South Wales 2484
Australia

Dear Mrs Singh

I am writing on behalf of the Prime Minister to acknowledge your recent letter and enclosed $5.

Pleased find enclosed a photograph of the Prime Minister. I am returning your $5 for your safekeeping.

Yours sincerely

S Caine

MR S CAINE

October 15, 2008

Office of Academic Human Resources
University of Illinois

NANCY SINGH (MRS)
PO Box 5067
South Murwillimbah
New South Wales 2484
Import and Export Services

Dear Sir,

I have been reading with great interest that your university has a special program for terrorists to become Professors.

One of my niece's sons is a member of the Tamil Tigers. He has decided that it is now time to lay low, get on with his life and get a good pension. He naturally thought that the program you offer would be suitable for him. He is much impressed by your employing the terrorist William Ayers.

I am writing in his stead as he is currently on the wanted list. Money is no problem and we are happy to pay for the necessary qualifications at your fine establishment. Please would you advise me on the best way to do this.

I am enclosing $5 to open our account in the meantime.

Sincerely,

Mrs. Nancy Singh

October 23, 2008

Senator Stephen Conroy

NANCY SINGH (MRS)
PO Box 5067
South Murwillimbah
New South Wales 2484
Import and Export Services

Dear Senator Conroy,

I see that you are calling for new board members for ABC and SBS, particularly people with 'a clear vision for public organisations engaged in the provision of broadcast services'. I think I can help.

Earlier this year I wrote to SBS offering such advice, clearly a 'challenge' in these shallow post-modern times. I pointed out that there is little to watch on SBS for us ladies. *Top Gear* for the boys is very good, but the Australian version is disappointing. I also think that SBS should get rid of all those foreign language films that nobody watches. As a migrant myself, the last thing I want to see is a load of moaning about multiculturalism.

As for the ABC, the last thing one should do is copy the BBC model, although I accept that Britain is generally better at these things than Australia. The BBC is now a bloated bureaucracy with four broadcast channels, satellite services, the World Service, six national radio stations and local radio as well. It employs more people than Robert Mugabe. It should be pared back to Radio 3 and 4 and BBC2, the rest is drivel. Our own ABC should be left (sic) as it is: one TV channel, Classic FM and Radio National. If it could rediscover unbiased journalism, that would also be welcome.

I hope these observations are of value. Let me know when we can meet to discuss remuneration.

Sincerely,

Mrs. Nancy Singh

October 23, 2008

NANCY SINGH (MRS)
PO Box 5067
South Murwillimbah
New South Wales 2484
Import and Export Services

Mr. Joel Fitzgibbon MP
Secretary for Defence

Dear Mr. Fitzgibbon,

I am writing to say how much I agree with your assessment of the 'challenge' in Afghanistan. It is not an easy place and frankly I don't think it is worth risking Australian lives for a bunch of barbarians. The Muslims have always treated their women appallingly, so really this should come as no surprise. I don't think a few women having to wear silly clothes is a good reason for Australia to go to war. It would be better to surrender and give it up now, like you did in Iraq.

I recall your remark about eating a few Mandarins in your time. This was very funny. I am wondering if you would send me a photo of your good self. I am enclosing $5 to cover postage.

Sincerely,

Mrs. Nancy Singh

October 23, 2008

NANCY SINGH (MRS)
PO Box 5067
South Murwillimbah
New South Wales 2484
Import and Export Services

Miss Julia Gillard MP
Minister for Productivity, Education and Socialism

Dear Miss Gillard,

I am disappointed that you have not replied to my letters. I know that you have been very busy trying to cover up the mess Mr. Swan and the Federal Reserve have made of the economy, but I had not taken you for the sort who would pocket $5 meant for postage.

Since it seems you are not willing to send me a signed photograph of you as requested, could I please have my $5 back?

Sincerely,

Mrs. Nancy Singh

October 23, 2008

NANCY SINGH (MRS)
PO Box 5067
South Murwillimbah
New South Wales 2484
Import and Export Services

Mr. John Murphy MP
Parliamentary Secretary
Canberra
ACT

Dear Mr. Murphy,

I hope you have had satisfaction in the 'Beef Stroganoff' affair. I see that the matter was fully debated by a Parliamentary Committee, as is quite proper. We cannot have our representatives fainting from lack of food.

I was wondering if you would send me a photo of yourself and your lovely wife. I am enclosing $5 to cover the postage.

Sincerely,

Mrs. Nancy Singh

October 23, 2008

NANCY SINGH (MRS)
PO Box 5067
South Murwillimbah
New South Wales 2484
Import and Export Services

Mr. Kevin Rude MP
Prime Minister

Dear Mr. Rudd,

I am disappointed that you have now failed to reply to three letters. Please will you return the $5 I sent you.

Sincerely,

Mrs. Nancy Singh

October 23, 2008

NANCY SINGH (MRS)
PO Box 5067
South Murwillimbah
New South Wales 2484
Import and Export Services

Mr. Lindsay Tanner
Minister for Finance

Dear Mr. Tanner,

I assure you I have no wish to say 'I told you so', but I told you so. The economy is now in a right old mess with growth slowing dramatically, unemployment rising and inflation accelerating all at the same time. Mr. Singh says that no one has managed to pull this off since Jimmy Carter. We had an idiot called Denis Healey in Britain around the same time.

My advice is to stop panicking and interfering in things governments do not understand. After all, it was the Fannie Mae fiasco that caused the banking collapse at root. If you can correct the banking collapse, then the economy will recover without the need to shovel money out like confetti to ungrateful teenagers and grannies. The trick to this is excising the bad debt that has cascaded through the banks. Bankers, of course, are to blame too, but they were told that the Mortgage Backed Securities they were buying were guaranteed by the US Government. Governments should be there to help the innocent, not to bail out stupidity and corruption.

I have to say that Mr. Swan does not inspire much confidence, he is clearly out of his depth and doesn't even follow your advice to say nothing. Mr. Rudd also appears to be increasingly dictatorial – perhaps I mean Presidential – and I worry that his moral compass is unbalanced.

You of course are much more balanced and clearly know what you are doing. The Opposition respects you too. So why not launch your own leadership bid? I think Mr. Rudd might well get fed up, pack it in and go to live in China.

Sincerely,

Mrs. Nancy Singh

October 23, 2008

Mr. Malcolm Turnbull MP

NANCY SINGH (MRS)
PO Box 5067
South Murwillimbah
New South Wales 2484
Import and Export Services

Dear Mr. Turnbull,

I know we have had our differences in the past, but I would like to put myself forward as one of your policy advisors. On the economy, I remain pro free markets and private investment; on social policy I am fairly conservative and would like to see welfare cut; I am an AWG skeptic; and I would take education policy in the direction of greater choice. I am a mature lady, not some green-behind-the-ears youngster like Mr. Epstein. I have a degree in Economics from the LSE and a diploma in Sociology.

Please let me know when I can start. I am happy to move to Canberra.

Sincerely,

Mrs. Nancy Singh

The Hon Malcolm Turnbull MP

LEADER OF THE OPPOSITION
MEMBER FOR WENTWORTH

11 November 2008

Mrs Nancy Singh
PO BOX 5067
South Murwillumbah NSW 2484

Dear Mrs Singh,

I attach the signed photograph of me that you requested.

Australia faces very challenging times and more than ever a strong Opposition is required to hold the Government accountable.

My colleagues and I are determined to provide Australia with the political and economic leadership it deserves as we work towards a return to Government in 2010.

Thank you for contacting my office and I hope you enjoy the photograph.

Yours sincerely,

Malcolm Turnbull MP

Parliament House Canberra ACT 2600 • Telep...
PO Box 1840 Bondi Junction NSW 1355 • Telephone (02) 9...

October 24, 2008

Miss Cate Blanchett
Sydney Theatre Company

NANCY SINGH (MRS)
PO Box 5067
South Murwillimbah
New South Wales 2484
Import and Export Services

Dear Miss Blanchett,

I am disappointed that you have not replied to my letter of 20th September. I know you are very busy and important, and I am just a common working woman but I had hoped for a better display of manners.

Since you are not prepared to send me a photo as requested, may I please have my $5 back …

Sincerely,

Mrs. Nancy Singh

October 24, 2008

NANCY SINGH (MRS)
PO Box 5067
South Murwillimbah
New South Wales 2484
Import and Export Services

Director of TV Entertainment
ABC

REMINDER

INVOICE

To the supply of humorous material:

$1000 only.

Sincerely,

Mrs. Nancy Singh

October 24, 2008

Mrs. Belinda Neal MP

NANCY SINGH (MRS)
PO Box 5067
South Murwillimbah
New South Wales 2484
Import and Export Services

Dear Mrs. Neal,

I am writing to congratulate you on getting off on the charge that you lied to Parliament. Although you can clearly be heard saying 'You'll make your baby a demon', it is obvious that your comments were taken out of 'context'.

I note that you have not sent me the photo I had asked for, so would ask you please to send my $5 back.

Sincerely,

Mrs. Nancy Singh

October 24, 2008

Mrs. Jacqui Smith MP
Home Secretary

NANCY SINGH (MRS)
PO Box 5067
South Murwillimbah
New South Wales 2484
Import and Export Services

Dear Mrs. Smith,

I saw you on the BBC yesterday, explaining that the increase in violent crime is all the fault of the police for logging crimes in the wrong categories. This is not very convincing, but I am prepared to keep an open mind until I have read the relevant report myself.

Please would you send me a copy of the latest British Crime Survey? I am enclosing $5 to cover postage.

Sincerely,

Mrs. Nancy Singh

Home Office

Direct Communications Unit
2 Marsham Street, London SW1P 4DF
Switchboard 020 7035 4848 Fax: 020 7035 4745 Textphone: 020 7035 4742
E-mail: public.enquiries@homeoffice.gsi.gov.uk Website: www.homeoffice.gov.uk

Mrs N Singh
PO BOX 5067
South Murwillimbah
New South Wales 2484

Reference: T23964/8

13 November 2008

Dear Mrs Singh,

Thank you for your letter of 24 October. I am sorry to hear of your disappointment at not receiving a response to your previous letters.

As I am sure you will appreciate, the Home Secretary receives a large number of letters and is unable to respond to each one individually. Therefore, your letter has been transferred to the Direct Communications Unit and I have been asked to reply. I am pleased to say a response was sent on 17 October and I hope you will have received this by now.

Thank you for sending the Home Office five Australian Dollars, to cover the cost of postage for receiving a hard-copy of the latest British Crime Survey. Whilst this is a much appreciated gesture we have the pleasure in returning this to you. The Home Office will cover the cost of sending you the report, which you will find enclosed.

Yours sincerely,

J Shockledge

J Shockledge (Miss)

November 3, 2008

Mr. John Brumby
Premier, Victoria

NANCY SINGH (MRS)
PO Box 5067
South Murwillimbah
New South Wales 2484
Import and Export Services

Dear Mr. Brumby,

I am writing to congratulate you on your stand in support of Dr. Moeller and his family in their application for permanent residency. It is quite disgraceful that such a fine, decent family should be treated in this cruel way and refused residency because their son is Down's Syndrome. I think Mrs. Sarah Palin would also be shocked, God bless her.

I believe you recently pointed out that Adelaide is a backwater. As you will know, Adelaide is the centre for processing residency applications. Having lived there myself for a brief but miserable period, I agree with you that Adelaidians are much more retarded than a Down's Syndrome Child and much less friendly. It is also the serial killer capital of Australia.

It is difficult to escape the conclusion that Dr. Moeller would have been better off arriving from Indonesia by boat and converting to Islam.

Sincerely,

Mrs. Nancy Singh

November 3, 2008

NANCY SINGH (MRS)
PO Box 5067
South Murwillimbah
New South Wales 2484
Import and Export Services

Director General
BBC
Bush House
London

Dear Sir,

One of your admin assistants has written to me in reply to my letter of 14th September, a Mr. David Shields. It seems he was too busy sitting about and drinking tea to simply post a photograph of Mr. Jeremy Paxman as requested. No matter.

I should have thought that you would be straining every sinew to win goodwill from the public and taxpayers following the recent scandals involving the BBC – cheating on kiddies, telephone call-ins, and now filth or so-called humour by Messrs Ross and Brand. We cannot have people claiming to have f****d other people's granddaughters, willy nilly, over the airwaves. I am surprised that you cannot see this, but then I understand that you are one of Lord Mandelson's gophers.

I shall be writing to Mr. David Cameron to urge him to cut the BBC down to size, back to the good old days of BBC2, Radio 3, Radio 4 and the radio version of the World Service. The BBC has had its day.

Sincerely,

Mrs. Nancy Singh

November 3, 2008

NANCY SINGH (MRS)
PO Box 5067
South Murwillimbah
New South Wales 2484
Import and Export Services

Mr. Chris Evans MP
Minister for Immigration

Dear Mr. Evans,

I refer to the appalling case of the Moeller family and the Australian government's disgraceful decision to refuse them permanent residency because their 13-year-old son is Down's Syndrome. My friends and family in the UK and USA agree that this shows Australia in a very bad light, worse even than Tamsin Lewis and the Australian cricket team. Some say it reminds them of eugenics in the 1930s, supported by socialists like H. G. Wells and Sidney Webb, not to mention the Germans.

This is a shame because we can be reasonably certain that Dr. Moeller is properly qualified, unlike that fake Arab 'doctor' in Queensland, and is not a Muslim terrorist. Perhaps your department would help him submit a new application as a refugee from Palestine or Iran in order to expedite a speedier resolution of this unsavoury incident.

Sincerely,

Mrs. Nancy Singh

Australian Government

Department of Immigration and Citizenship

Mrs Nancy Singh
PO Box 5067
SOUTH MURWILLUMBAH NSW 2484

Dear Mrs Singh

Thank you for your letter of 03 November 2008 regarding the refusal of an Employer Nomination Scheme (Subclass 856) visa for Dr Bernard Moeller and his family. The Minister has asked that I respond on his behalf. I regret the delay in responding.

On 26 November 2008, the Minister for Immigration and Citizenship, Senator Chris Evans, granted Dr Moeller and his family permanent residence. Compelling considerations were the valuable contribution Dr Moeller's family is making to the Horsham community, given the severe shortage of rural doctors, and the substantial community support.

I appreciate that you were disappointed at the initial decision by the Department of Immigration and Citizenship. The Moeller family were also understandably disappointed given their desire to reside in Australia. However, all permanent visa applicants are required to meet the relevant criteria for grant of a visa, and the Department is required to apply the rules equally to all cases. This includes meeting Australia's health requirement.

The health requirement, which is a long standing government policy, is designed to minimise any risk to public health, ensure that public health expenditure on health and community services is contained and Australian residents' access to health and other community services in short supply is maintained.

In this case, as part of the visa application process, Dr Moeller's son was assessed by a Medical Officer of the Commonwealth (MOC) as being unable to meet the health requirement because his condition was likely to result in significant costs to the Australian community if a permanent visa were to be granted.

Once this assessment was made the visa decision-maker was required to refuse the visa application. This is because under Australian migration law a MOC's opinion must be taken as correct. Hence, it would have been unlawful for the decision-maker to override this opinion. No discretion is available to the decision-maker under migration law.

I can assure you that the initial decision by the Department to refuse Dr Moeller's visa application was not because of discrimination against individuals with Down syndrome – it is a matter of likely costs to the Australia community. A disability is not, in itself, a ground for failing the health requirement for migration.

Active Tuberculosis is the only condition that automatically precludes the grant of a visa. All other conditions such as kidney disease, cancer or heart disease are assessed against the same criteria (that is, likely costs to the community and likely prejudice to Australians' access to required health and community services in short supply) to determine whether an affected applicant is able to meet the health requirement.

The Minister also announced that in consultation with the Parliamentary Secretary, The Hon Bill Shorten, Disabilities and Children's Services, he has asked the Joint Standing Committee on Migration to look at the issue of people with a disability in context of the migration health requirement.

Thank you for bringing this matter to our attention.

Yours sincerely

Kruno Kukoc
First Assistant Secretary
Principal Advisor Migration Strategies
Migration and Visa Policy Division

12 December 2008

November 3, 2008

NANCY SINGH (MRS)
PO Box 5067
South Murwillimbah
New South Wales 2484
Import and Export Services

Miss Jenny Macklin MP
Minister for Families, Housing, Community Services and Indigenous Affairs

Dear Miss Macklin,

Thank you for your reply to my letter of 27th August, which arrived today. I hope your civil servants are a bit quicker at helping the poor old Aborigines than this!

I apologise for not having used your full title in my earlier letters. It is a bit of a long 'handle', and does not lend itself to an acronym as so widely used by the government, such as GUESS or the Government's Economic Security Strategy.

I wish you well in your endeavours to introduce more Aborigines to the work ethic and the self-respect that comes with a job. I note, however, that since your government has come to office employment is falling and unemployment rising. I knew a Labor government would ruin the economy and blow the surplus, but I had thought it would have taken longer than nine months.

Sincerely,

Mrs. Nancy Singh

November 3, 2008

Mr. Rupert Murdoch
Sky News

NANCY SINGH (MRS)
PO Box 5067
South Murwillimbah
New South Wales 2484
Import and Export Services

Dear Mr. Murdoch,

Welcome back to your homeland. I watched excerpts from your recent speech on the 'bludger' tradition here in Australia, or 'dole bums' as we used to say in the UK. I think you are right about this, and see that Mr. Rudd's experiment in welfare socialism will set us back many years just as Tony Blair ruined Britain. I also agree with you that the election of Barack Obama will make the recession much deeper and longer-lasting.

It is too late now to complain of craven bias in the news media in the coverage of Messrs Obama and McCain, with the noble exception of Fox News. I tell you, it has been just as bad here in Australia; I can't think of a single TV station or newspaper that prefers Mr. McCain. Your own Sky News has been a disgrace, but then they also helped Mr. Rudd to be elected. I have decided to cancel my subscription to Sky News and CNN, which is almost as bad.

Perhaps you could have a quiet word and hopefully sack a few lefties.

Sincerely,

Mrs. Nancy Singh

November 3, 2008

NANCY SINGH (MRS)
PO Box 5067
South Murwillimbah
New South Wales 2484
Import and Export Services

Mrs. Jacqui Smith MP
Home Secretary

Dear Mrs. Smith,

Thank you for your letter of 17 October, sent by Mrs. M Lockmun of the Home Office Direct Communications Unit. It is a pity that my original letter has gone astray, but the urgency of the situation has now subsided.

Our query was in relation to the 'Stab Vest' you wear when outdoors on Britain's violent streets. Mr. Singh and I had intended to purchase a pair of these items to wear during an enforced return visit to West London. Mr. Singh's brother was gravely ill, but has since made a remarkable recovery.

However, as we have a good many relatives in the UK I expect we will be back again next year for some reason or other. So if you could send me the name of the manufacturer or retailer of your stab vest that would be very helpful indeed. I am enclosing $5 to cover the postage.

Sincerely,

Mrs. Nancy Singh

Home Office

Direct Communications Unit
2 Marsham Street, London SW1P 4DF
Switchboard 020 7035 4848 Fax: 020 7035 4745 Textphone: 020 7035 4742
E-mail: public.enquiries@homeoffice.gsi.gov.uk Website: www.homeoffice.gov.uk

Mrs Nancy Singh
PO Box 5067
South Murwillimbah
New South Wales 2484
Australia

Reference: T24708/8

22 December 2008

Dear Mrs Singh,

Thank you for your letter of 3 November to the Home Secretary about buying a stab vest. As I am sure you will appreciate, the Home Secretary receives a large amount of correspondence and is unfortunately not able to respond to each letter individually. I have been asked to reply.

The Home Office cannot recommend which stab-proof vest you should buy. If you wish to buy a stab vest, I suggest that you look on the internet for further information on the type of manufacturers or retailers.

I return the $5 you enclosed with your previous letter.

Yours sincerely,

Miss C Johnson

November 3, 2008

NANCY SINGH (MRS)
PO Box 5067
South Murwillimbah
New South Wales 2484
Import and Export Services

Mr. Glenn Stevens,
Governor of the Federal Reserve Bank

Dear Mr. Stevens,

I am not one of those who would gloat and say 'I told you so', but I did in fact tell you so. A little bit of 'inflation' was much preferable to a recession as I think even you must now admit. The interest rate rises of 2006 and 2007 – especially the one in the middle of the general election – can now be seen for what they really were: panic measures and completely unnecessary.

I accept, of course, that the banking collapse has had an impact on spending, but the slowdown was already underway well before mid September. The banking collapse would have corrected without massive handouts from government, but in any event the 'real' economy will recover quickly. So it would be amusing to see Mr. Rudd panicking and throwing money about like confetti at a Mafia wedding, but of course he is making things worse instead of better. I bet you are regretting your role in bringing down the Howard government and its replacement by a load of shop stewards who lack the *nous* of a barrow boy.

We must all tighten our belts. If it is any comfort to you, things will be nowhere near as bad as 1989–92. Unless of course, another tropical cyclone damages the banana crop! Best wishes,

Sincerely,

Mrs. Nancy Singh

RESERVE BANK OF AUSTRALIA

65 Martin Place
GPO Box 3947
SYDNEY NSW 2001

Telephone (02) 9551 9701

Secretary's Department

http://www.rba.gov.au
Facsimile (02) 9551 8041
Email dickmana@rba.gov.au

In reply please quote SD
Filename D08/328882

17 November 2008

Mrs Nancy Singh
PO Box 5067
SOUTH MURWILLIMBAH NSW 2484

Dear Mrs Singh

The Governor of the Reserve Bank, Glenn Stevens, has asked me to acknowledge receipt of your letter of 3 November.

Yours sincerely

Anthony Dickman
Deputy Secretary

November 4, 2008

Proposed PhD Research: The Penile City

NANCY SINGH (MRS)
PO Box 5067
South Murwillimbah
New South Wales 2484
Import and Export Services

I wish to undertake PhD research on the subject of the Australian city, its development and built form from a Marxist-feminist, post-structuralist and post-colonial viewpoint. My hypothesis is that Australian cities are steeped in a history of penal cruelty, ignorance, sexism and racism. This can be seen, at the surface level, in the laying out of streets to a strict grid pattern by white male colonialists. However, beneath the surface all manner of atrocities and injustices lurk such as in the case of Darlinghurst Prison being run as a brothel, the expulsion of Aborigines from the cities – beyond Boundary Street, the wide-spread child sex abuse in Adelaide and the persecution of the Gay, Lesbian, Bi-sexual, Transsexual and Queer Community in Sydney. Underlying all of this is a deep-rooted sexism and fear of the other.

The research will be based on historical sources and feminist literature. Chapters will include: early settlements, the criminal classes and prostitution; fascisistic male city planning in the 19th century; the brothel pogroms of the 1950s; the design of new towns as controlled environments for the subjugation of women; market forces and little boxes – the suburbs and the cult of wife-swapping; serial sex-offenders and the Catholic Church – the case of Adelaide; sex, degeneracy and sleeping with the enemy in 1960s Sydney; the legitimization of male sexual deviance by the legalizing of brothels; women, the creative industries and sex slavery; gay-bashing in Sydney's eastern suburbs; the threat of global warming, peak oil and its impacts on immigration and female bondage; the growth of the catalogue bride industry and its consequences for sustainability in developing countries; sex – the new Chinese export; the end of male tyranny.

I hope to conclude with a discussion of how to dismantle the Penile City and replace it with a true community based on female virtues – the Vaginal City, multi-culturalism and the ascendancy of secular Islam, genuine sustainability and controlled breeding: Identity, Community, Stability.

Sincerely,

Mrs. Nancy Singh

THE UNIVERSITY OF
MELBOURNE

MELBOURNE
SCHOOL OF
GRADUATE
RESEARCH

19-Nov-08

Mrs Nancy Singh
PO Box 5067
South Murwillimbah NSW 2484

Re: Proposed PhD Research: The Penile City

Dear Mrs Singh

Your letter dated 4 November 2008 has been forwarded to me by the Office of the Pro-Vice Chancellor. I have enquired about your application with the Melbourne School of Land & Environment (MSLE), who administer PhD applications for the School of Resource Management & Geography (the University does not have a School of Geography). Unfortunately MSLE have no record of receiving your PhD application.

If you wish to apply for PhD candidature at The University of Melbourne I would recommend that you resubmit your proposal, along with a PhD Application Form (enclosed), to The Graduate Studies Office, Melbourne School of Land and Environment.

PhD applicants are also strongly encouraged to make contact with prospective supervisors directly prior to submitting an application. Information on current research and academic staff contact details are available on the MSLE website, http://www.landfood.unimelb.edu.au/info/staff.html.

The University's Research Report is also an excellent source of information on current research and researchers: http://www.research.unimelb.edu.au/rpag/reports/research/, as is the Find an Expert facility: http://www.findanexpert.unimelb.edu.au/index.html

My apologies for any inconvenience or distress you have experienced in attempting to apply for PhD candidature at The University of Melbourne. Best of luck with your future endeavours.

Kind regards

A. McAulay

Alex McAulay
Admissions Officer

Melbourne School of Graduate Research
The University of Melbourne Victoria 3010 Australia
T: +61 3 8344 8599 **F:** +61 3 9349 2103 **W:** www.gradstudies.unimelb.edu.au

ABN 40 000 382 669

University of New South Wales Press Ltd

POSTAL ADDRESS UNSW Sydney NSW 2052 Australia
COURIERS AND VISITORS 45 Beach Street Coogee NSW 2034

www.unswpress.com.au

6 November 2008

Mrs N Singh
PO Box 5067
Murwillimbah
NSW 2484

Dear Mrs Singh

RE: *The Penile City*

Thank you for submitting your book proposal to UNSW Press for publishing consideration.

Unfortunately, your project is not suitable for our list, and we enclose your $5 herewith.

Thank you all the same for giving us the opportunity to consider this. We wish you every success in securing a suitable publisher.

Yours sincerely

Publishing Department
UNSW Press

PROFESSOR JOAN COOPER
PRO-VICE-CHANCELLOR
(STUDENTS) AND REGISTRAR

10 November 2008

Mrs Nancy Singh
PO Box 5067
MURWILLIMBAH NSW 2484

Dear Mrs Singh,

In response to your letter to my office dated November 4 2008, I have spoken to UNSW Press and they have informed me your $5 cheque has now been returned to you.

Yours sincerely,

Joan Cooper

THE UNIVERSITY OF NEW SOUTH WALES
UNSW SYDNEY NSW 2052 AUSTRALIA
Telephone: +61 (2) 9385 1067
Facsimile: +61 (2) 9385 1385
Email: j.cooper@unsw.edu.au
ABN 57 195 873 179

University of
South Australia

30 November 2008

Mrs Nancy Singh
PO Box 5067
South Murwillimbah NSW 2484

Dear Mrs Singh

Thank you for your letter of 4 November addressed to our Pro Vice Chancellor concerning your proposal to undertake PhD research on the subject of the male dominance of city planning and design.

This section handles all applications for higher degrees by research.

We have checked our records and do not have any information that we received your application or the $5 you sent. We have an online application form and can assure you that we acknowledge all applications received and consider each on their academic merit.

Please don't hesitate to contact me if I can be of further assistance.

Best wishes for your research.

Yours sincerely

Jayne Taylor
Manager, Research Education & Training

Research & Innovation Services – Research Education & Training

GP2.12
Mawson Lakes
South Australia 5095

GPO Box 2471
Adelaide
South Australia 5001
Australia

t: +61 8 8302 3956
f: +61 8 8302 3997
jayne.taylor@unisa.edu.au

www.unisa.edu.au/research degrees

University of
South Australia

22 January 2009

Mrs Nancy Singh
PO Box 5067
South Murwillimbah NSW 2484

Dear Mrs Singh

Thank you for your letter of 21 December regarding your proposed research.

In order for us to assess you for entry into a Doctor of Philosophy program, you will need to complete an application form and provide evidence of previous study.

UniSA has an online application form which can be found at:
http://www.unisa.edu.au/resdegrees/howtoapply/default.asp

I have also enclosed a checklist for the series of steps that you will need to follow to enable you to complete the application.

Best wishes for your application.

Yours sincerely

Jayne Taylor
Manager, Research Education & Training

Research & Innovation Services – Research Education & Training

GP2.12
Mawson Lakes
South Australia 5095

GPO Box 2471
Adelaide
South Australia 5001
Australia

t: +61 8 8302 3956
f: +61 8 8302 3997
jayne.taylor@unisa.edu.au

www.unisa.edu.au/research degrees

November 4, 2008

NANCY SINGH (MRS)
PO Box 5067
South Murwillimbah
New South Wales 2484
Import and Export Services

Mr. Chris Bowen MP
Minister for the Treasury

Dear Mr. Bowen,

I am disappointed not to have received a reply from you to my letters of 14th August and 12th September. I can only conclude that you were sent to a school where they did not teach proper manners.

I see that Mr. Rudd has given you the task of defending the government's bungling in the banking sector. What on earth were you thinking of when you decided to give 100% guarantees to bank deposits? Mr. Singh and I cannot get access to our funds because of your mismanagement.

Is it true that the government's advice is to go along to Centrelink with all the bludgers, to use Mr. Rupert Murdoch's colourful language?

On another matter, I see that petrol prices have fallen a little in recent weeks, so it is clear that your *FuelWatch* initiative is working. Many congratulations on this small but important success.

Sincerely,

Mrs. Nancy Singh

November 12, 2008

NANCY SINGH (MRS)
PO Box 5067
South Murwillimbah
New South Wales 2484
Import and Export Services

Mr. Anthony Albanese MP
Minister for Infrastructure

Dear Mr. Albanese,

I am writing to say how worrying it is to see that the government is now blowing the budget surplus by throwing handouts about: old people, sulky teenagers, unmarried mothers, the car industry, ABC Learning, the banks, deposit accounts and other 'bludgers'. Being fiscal conservatives didn't last very long really.

The sad thing is that there will now be no money for infrastructure projects and other pork: bridges, tunnels, roads, railway lines, wharves and jetties, runways and whatever. This must be a bit of a disappointment for you. Still, it is probably a good thing in some ways, as I shouldn't trust the state governments to know what they are doing. New South Wales is a black hole when it comes to public finance and South Australia is a backwater.

It might be best to concentrate on building dams and sorting out water, as President Hoover did in the USA. The Hoover Dam still bears his name to this day. I hope this advice is helpful to you.

Sincerely,
Mrs. Nancy Singh

November 12, 2008

NANCY SINGH (MRS)
PO Box 5067
South Murwillimbah
New South Wales 2484
Import and Export Services

Miss Julia Gillard MP
Minister for Education, Employment and Workplace Relations

Dear Miss Gillard,

I thank you for the letter sent on your behalf by a Mr. Stewart Thomas. I am sorry I got the title of your portfolio wrong. For future reference, please would you note that my preferred salutation is Mrs., and not Ms. I am very proud of the fact that I am married to Mr. Singh.

I am writing anew because of the ABC Learning fiasco. I was wondering if they have gone bust because you yourself threatened them with unspecified action should they increase their prices. Clearly they did not increase their prices, and so are now bankrupt. Is this an example of Mr. Rudd's 'extreme capitalism' would you say, or a result of government intervention in market pricing?

Perhaps we could find a 'third way' out of this mess, by encouraging parents to take shares in their local childcare centre, and run it as a business themselves. Government could buy the buildings and rent them out, and perhaps provide a business development grant. The trouble is, while many parents are good at complaining and wanting the government to take responsibility, they are not so good at taking responsibility themselves or, indeed, of running businesses. They would probably go bankrupt too.

NANCY SINGH (MRS)
PO Box 5067
South Murwillimbah
New South Wales 2484
Import and Export Services

At this rate we shall all end up working for the government! Like ABC and the car industry, I have run up some debt myself which I am struggling to repay. I was wondering if the government would bail me out too? Where should I send my credit card statement to be reimbursed?

Sincerely,

Mrs. Nancy Singh

November 12, 2008

NANCY SINGH (MRS)
PO Box 5067
South Murwillimbah
New South Wales 2484
Import and Export Services

Mr. Mike Rann
Premier
South Australia

Dear Mr. Rann,

I am writing to say how pleased I am to see that someone at last has some vision for South Australia as a builder of nuclear submarines. Do not be side-tracked by those who argue that nuclear fission is dangerous. Indeed, there is a great future for SA not only in mining uranium and building submarines, but also in nuclear power. We can finally get all these moaning greenies off our backs. I myself have had radiation treatment and have never felt better.

I hope you will not mind my asking for a signed photograph of you. In these inflationary times I know that every penny matters, so here is $5 for the postage. Is it true that you shall be moving to Italy soon with your lovely wife?

Sincerely,

Mrs. Nancy Singh

November 12, 2008

NANCY SINGH (MRS)
PO Box 5067
South Murwillimbah
New South Wales 2484
Import and Export Services

Mr. Alex Salmon MSP
First Minister of Scotland

Dear Mr. Salmon,

I am writing to say how sorry I am that the SNP lost the Kirkcaldy bye-election so disastrously. You are getting the blame for the mess Tony Blair made of Scotland, especially as regards violent street crime and racial conflict, and filthy hospitals. I hope you are not worrying unduly about the common folk of Fife; I stayed there for a few months once and couldn't wait to leave again. The people there are worse than Bo'Nessians. It is hard to believe that Scotland once produced the likes of Adam Smith, Lord Kames and David Hume, James Watt and Henry Bell.

I also believe some of the nonsense that passes for debate in the Scottish Parliament is working against you. A good (that is bad) example is the question of allowing homosexuals to give blood. This is being debated as a 'right', which of course is just silly and post-modern; when the truth is that *louche* behaviour increases the risk of AIDS. I know a good man when I see one. You should stick to your guns and don't give in to the far-left homo-sexualists.

It might be an idea to sack a few ministers to let the people know who is to blame for high taxes, too-high immigration, knife crime, loony local councils, fly-tipping and the closure of post offices. But overall I am gloomy that Scotland has become a socialist welfare state basket case, in marked contrast to Ireland.

NANCY SINGH (MRS)
PO Box 5067
South Murwillimbah
New South Wales 2484
Import and Export Services

I was wondering if you would send me a photo of your good self. In these days of the credit crunch, I know every penny counts, so am enclosing $5 to cover the postage.

Sincerely,

Mrs. Nancy Singh

November 12, 2008

Mr. Jack Straw MP

NANCY SINGH (MRS)
PO Box 5067
South Murwillimbah
New South Wales 2484
Import and Export Services

Dear Mr. Straw,

I have been an admirer of your cautious brand of politics for many years, and at one point was one of your constituents. We were very proud of you holding your end up with Dr. Condoleeza Rice.

I now live in Australia. Mr. Singh and I became afraid of street crime, racial thuggery, violence and nutty Muslims in the UK. It is not safe for Hindus now. Is it true that there are now 5 million Muslims in the UK, that 80% want Sharia Law and about 50,000 are training as suicide bombers? No wonder Tony Blair has left the country! I fear that Western civilization itself is now under threat. So it is good to see you at last standing up to Islamic extremists. But I fear it is too late, as in Holland and Belgium and France.

I am enclosing $5 to cover postage as I should be most grateful if you would send me a signed photo of your charming self.

Sincerely,

Mrs. Nancy Singh

Ministry of Justice
102 Petty France
London SW1H 9AJ

www.justice.gov.uk

Mrs Singh,
Money for postage returned.
Many thanks.
Carine

With Compliments

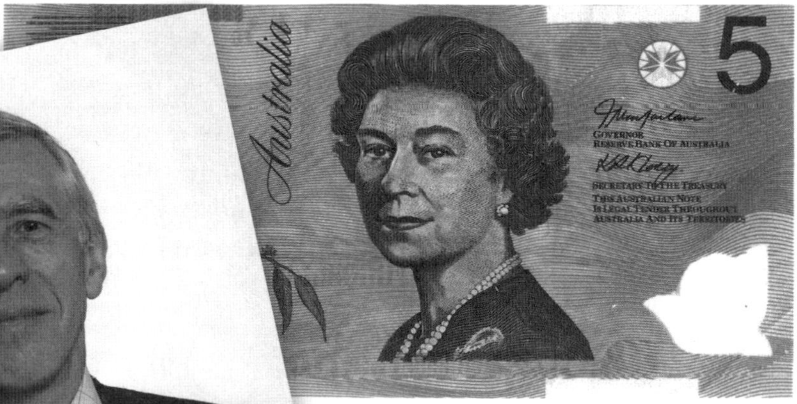

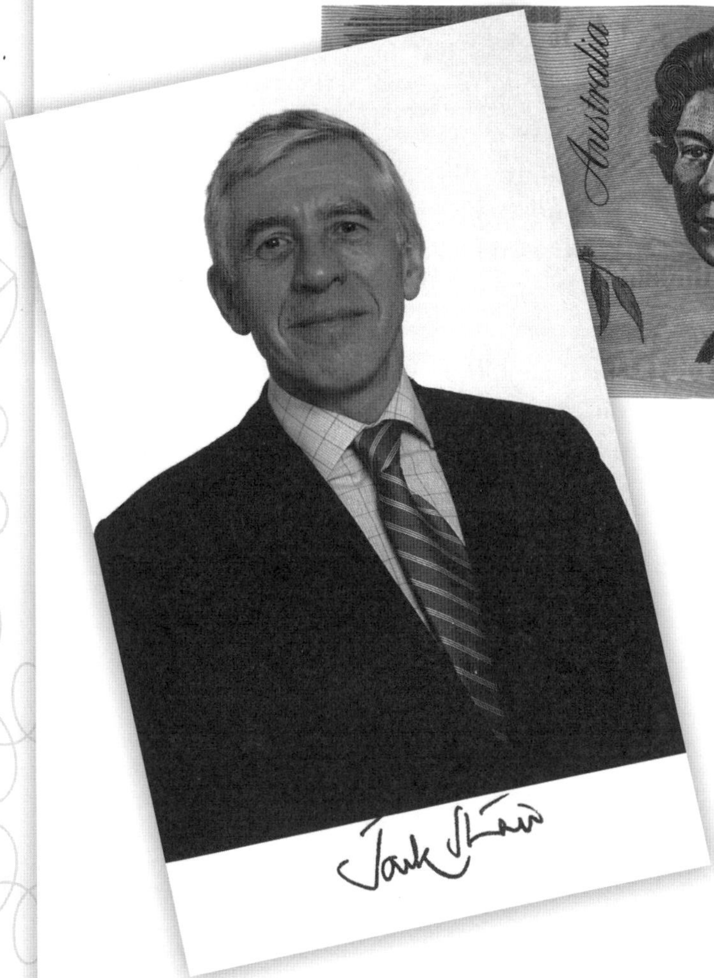

November 17, 2008

NANCY SINGH (MRS)
PO Box 5067
South Murwillimbah
New South Wales 2484
Import and Export Services

Rt. Hon. Kevin Rudd MP
Prime Minister of Australia

Dear Mr. Rudd,

I like a good joke as much as the next person, and see nothing wrong with you pointing out to all and sundry that President George W. Bush is a complete imbecile who doesn't even know what the G30 is. I am sure the damage done to US–Australian relations is repairable.

I am impressed by your handling of the GLOBAL FINANCIAL CRISIS and the GATHERING ECONOMIC STORM, and the various other CHALLENGES you refer to every day. A word of caution though, it is possible to throw too much money at these problems, bankrupt the government and set off inflation all over again. But this time you will be unable to blame Mr. John Howard.

As a newcomer to this great land, I am taken aback by the rudeness displayed during Question Time in Parliament. Is it really necessary for you to refer to your opponents as 'the three stoogies', 'chavs and spivs', or Mr. Malcolm Turnbull as the 'Merchant of Venice' or the 'Member for Goldman Sachs'? I even overheard someone call the splendid Joe Hockey a 'fat, greasy b*****d'!

I worry that the Opposition might retaliate and refer to you as the Prime Kept Man, Mr. Rude or the Member for the Moaning Classes. This would be highly regrettable and insulting to voters' intelligence.

I hope you find these well-intended words of advice helpful.

Sincerely,

Mrs. Nancy Singh

December 11, 2008

NANCY SINGH (MRS)
PO Box 5067
South Murwillimbah
New South Wales 2484
Import and Export Services

Dr. Helen Szoke
CEO
Equal Opportunities Commission

Dear Dr. Szoke,

I read with interest your proposal that there should be positive discrimination against white males. I think this is an excellent idea, as it will continue the practice of employing women and black people, homosexuals and Muslims at every opportunity. True, in practice this has often proved disastrous as competent people are often replaced or overlooked for PC reasons. But that is a price worth paying, as I am sure you agree.

I wonder if this could be taken further, in the interests of reducing violence and male bawdiness in society. I am sure I speak for the many students of Caucasian Studies who believe that white men should be bred out of existence. This could be achieved in a generation or two by a humane program of sterilisation. There would be no more blondes and no more blue eyes, everyone would be an attractive shade of brown.

There would of course be no artists to speak of, great inventors or entrepreneurs, but we have probably had enough of all of this anyway. There would be no one to protect us from the Muslim fanatics, but I guess women could operate the atomic bomb by laptop and so take care of that.

I was wondering if you have a policy paper setting out your vision for a society without white men? I am enclosing $5 for postage in the hope that you will send me a copy.

Sincerely,

Mrs. Nancy Singh

Victorian Equal Opportunity
& Human Rights Commission

www.humanrightscommission.vic.gov.au

Mrs. Nancy Singh
PO Box 5067
South Murwillimbah
NSW 2484

9th January 2009

Dear Mrs Singh,
Thank-you for your letter dated December 11 2008, which I presume is regarding the piece in the Herald Sun - *Jobs push for the marginalised - White men can go jump*, by Susie O'Brien.

The article's headline and opening paragraphs inaccurately stated that discrimination against "white males" would soon be encouraged as part of proposed changes to the Equal Opportunity Act.

This is incorrect and in fact contrary to the principles of equal opportunity laws.

Comments attributed to the Commission's CEO, Dr Helen Szoke, were also incorrectly reported out of context.

The Commission has relayed its concerns to the reporter and the Herald Sun and received an assurance that the errors will not be repeated.

I am returning the $5 you enclosed.

Yours Sincerely

Scott

Slavka Scott
Projects and Communications Manager
Victorian Equal Opportunity & Human Rights Commission

January 20, 2009

Mrs. Quentin Bryce
Governor General of Australia

NANCY SINGH (MRS)
PO Box 5067
South Murwillimbah
New South Wales 2484
Import and Export Services

Dear Mrs. Bryce,

I am writing to tell you how moved I was by the award of the Victoria Cross to that young soldier. Bless them all.

I thought you were very elegant and dignified, although I am not sure the colour pink was entirely appropriate because of its association with Code Pink and other nasty militant lesbian stirrers. Still, it is clear that the suit is an old favourite of yours. It is only right and proper that you should feel comfortable in your dress.

I was wondering if you would send me a photograph of the event or perhaps an official portrait of your good self. It does us proud that you are our GG. I am enclosing $5 to cover the cost of postage.

Sincerely,

Mrs. Nancy Singh

OFFICE OF THE OFFICIAL SECRETARY
TO THE GOVERNOR-GENERAL

Mrs Nancy Singh
PO Box 5067
SOUTH MURWILLIMBAH NSW 2848

Dear Mrs Singh

Thank you for your letter of 17 November 2008 to the Governor-General requesting a knighthood for your husband.

I am sorry to disappoint you, but it has been the policy of successive governments that the honours system no longer provides for awards that bestow prefixes or titles including knighthoods. Therefore I am returning your five dollars.

The Government considers that the current honours arrangements, particularly the appointments that are provided for by the Order of Australia, allow for the achievement and service of our fellow Australians to be appropriately and publicly acknowledged and recognised.

More information about the Australian Honours System, including nominations forms can be found on the Awards and Culture Branch website at www.itsanhonour.gov.au.

Yours sincerely

Brien Hallett
Deputy Official Secretary to the Governor-General

12 December 2008

GOVERNMENT HOUSE CANBERRA ACT 2600 AUSTRALIA
TELEPHONE (02) 6283 3533 FACSIMILE (02) 6281 3760 WEBSITE www.gg.gov.au

January 20, 2009

Miss Nicola Roxon MP
Minister for Health

NANCY SINGH (MRS)
PO Box 5067
South Murwillimbah
New South Wales 2484
Import and Export Services

Dear Miss Roxon,

I find it ironic that you are now complaining because some enterprising drinks company is producing bottled mixers with a beer base. I had thought you would have heard of the 'law of unintended consequences' and the fact that people react badly to petty bans and unfair governance. Just because you are a Minister gives you no right to boss people about and tell us how to run our lives. Three cheers to the drinks industry: sip, sip, hooray!

I know you had an alcoholic in your family, but the rest of us are quite content to tipple and take our minds off idiotic politicians, economists and know-nothing women television presenters. Please can you just leave us in peace.

I doubt very much that in your days as a Doc Marten wearing girly feminist you would have taken kindly to some dowdy middle-aged woman telling you what to do. Perhaps you need to lighten up a little and pay more attention to your hair, make-up and dress sense. It is all very well buying clothes from op shops, but the key is to buy only classic items.

Sincerely,

Mrs. Nancy Singh

January 20, 2009

NANCY SINGH (MRS)
PO Box 5067
South Murwillimbah
New South Wales 2484
Import and Export Services

Mrs. Kevin Rudd
First Lady of Australia
C/o Mr. Kevin Rudd, Prime Minister

Dear Mrs. Rudd,

I am writing to say how nice it was to see you at the Boxing Day Test Match in Sydney. Mr. Singh and I are cricket enthusiasts.

I was a little surprised that you chose such an ill-fitting linen suit. I suppose Mr. Rudd is a bit mean with the housekeeping money, as befits one of lower middle class ambitions. For a moment I thought you had donated your skirt for use as a makeshift bowling screen, but then realised this was cobbled together from a pair of old sheets. I am sure you would have helped out if called upon!

Mr. Rudd does look so much happier when he is abroad, doesn't he? I hope he doesn't overlook the sensible running of the country – as did his apogee Tony Blair who left Britain to be taken over by the PC brigade and violent Muslim extremists. Australia is not so bad, as long as we keep the Muslims out.

Sincerely,

Mrs. Nancy Singh

January 20, 2009

Mr. Alex Salmond MSP
First Minister of Scotland

NANCY SINGH (MRS)
PO Box 5067
South Murwillimbah
New South Wales 2484
Import and Export Services

Dear Mr. Salmond,

I do apologise for getting your name wrong in my previous letter. Your Miss Fraser, a somewhat officious admin assistant, has written to pull me up on that score. I expect you all refer to her as Miss Bossy.

The point I was making is to do with public health. It is well known that homosexuals are more sexually active, and have many more partners, than heterosexuals. Also, anal intercourse is much more risky than using a woman's yoni. I believe the Surgeon General has made this very point himself. So it is not a question of 'human rights' but simply a matter of good public health management.

I have no problem with homosexuals doing whatever it is they do, in private. What I object to is the noisy leftards shouting their faces off about so-called human rights every five minutes. I also oppose 'gay' marriage. But I say live and let live, that is the best way.

NANCY SINGH (MRS)
PO Box 5067
South Murwillimbah
New South Wales 2484
Import and Export Services

As you are a Nationalist, I have no idea whether you are a Conservative, Socialist or perhaps a Classical Liberal. My only observation is that socialism has been bad for Scotland, whereas Ireland is doing very well from a liberal market economy and a strong sense of identity and tradition. Scotland needs to get the far left off its back.

I hope you find these few words helpful. A Merry Christmas to you and a bonny New Year.

Sincerely,

Mrs. Nancy Singh

January 20, 2009

Mr. Glenn Stevens,
Governor of the Federal Reserve Bank

NANCY SINGH (MRS)
PO Box 5067
South Murwillimbah
New South Wales 2484
Import and Export Services

Dear Mr. Stevens,

Someone from your office very kindly replied to my previous letter on the banking collapse and the economic downturn. But they didn't seem to know very much about either.

I am writing to wish you a happy new year and every success in your new career. I am sure it will not be long now before you do the decent thing by resigning over the mess you have made of our economy. Less than a year ago you were complaining about inflation and putting up interest rates, even although we in the real world of business could see that the economy was already grinding to a halt. The downturn was well underway by July, long before the collapse of Lehman Brothers.

As I have said to you before, I also think that Mr. Greenspan and Mr. Bernanke made crucial mistakes in raising rates in 2006 and 2007. I think it would be better for us all if economists found something else to do and left the economy to wealth creators and businessmen.

But no hard feelings. Good luck in your new role, whatever that may be.

Sincerely,

Mrs. Nancy Singh

January 20, 2009

NANCY SINGH (MRS)
PO Box 5067
South Murwillimbah
New South Wales 2484
Import and Export Services

Mr. Lindsay Tanner
Minister for Finance

Dear Mr. Tanner,

I am prepared to accept the post of Media Assistant under certain conditions. The first is that you tone down all that nasty schoolboy behaviour that passes for debate in the Parliament. My mother always told me you cannot trust a man with a potty mouth.

Second, I think you should call for Mr. Glenn Stevens, the Reserve Bank Governor, to resign for his sheer incompetence in causing the downturn. I can see why you, as a politician, would try to play this down and blame everything on the Global Financial Crisis, but the truth is that the economy was already on the slide in July, before the collapse of Lehman's. Even Blind Freddy can see this, and so too can little Nancy Singh.

Would the post be based in Melbourne or Canberra? I confess I find both of them cold and dreary, but would put up with this to work for such a strong and attractive man.

Sincerely,

Mrs. Nancy Singh

March 21, 2009

Miss Sharon Burrows
Secretary of the ACTU

NANCY SINGH (MRS)
PO Box 5067
South Murwillimbah
New South Wales 2484
Import and Export Services

Dear Miss Burrows,

I am writing to congratulate you over your success in introducing Fair Work Australia. This will show those hateful small business owners!

As you know, Mr Singh and I have a collection of businesses, although we are not as wealthy as Mr. and Mrs. Rudd, or Mr. Peter Garrett for that matter. We are naturally concerned about the so-called unfair dismissal clauses, and the fact that trade union officials will now be able to enter our premises and search through our files. We might have to keep our records in my panty drawer.

Mr Singh and I are now preparing to cut staff numbers in each of our businesses down to 15 as the Union Movement dictates. This is a pity, as we think of ourselves and our staff as a family. But it only takes one bad apple, as you will know from your dealings with Miss Belinda Neal. (In passing, I wonder why it is that so many women on the left are hard-faced and unattractive?)

I feel I ought to warn you that there will be many more job losses as a result of your short-sighted actions.

Sincerely,

Mrs. Nancy Singh

NO RESPONSE

March 21, 2009

NANCY SINGH (MRS)
PO Box 5067
South Murwillimbah
New South Wales 2484
Import and Export Services

Miss Julia Gillard MP
Minister for Education, Employment and Workplace Relations and Social Exclusion

Dear Miss Gillard,

I am writing to congratulate you over your success in introducing Fair Work Australia. This will show those hateful small business owners!

As you know, Mr Singh and I have a collection of businesses, although we are not as wealthy as Mr and Mrs Rudd. We are naturally concerned about the so-called unfair dismissal clauses. I should be grateful if you would send me a copy of the section of your Bill that deals with these matters, and am enclosing $5 to cover postage.

Mr Singh and I are now preparing to cut staff numbers in each of our businesses down to 15 as the State dictates. This is a pity, as we think of ourselves and our staff as a family. But it only takes one bad apple, as you will know from your dealings with Brian Burke, or for that matter the disasterous 'leadership' of Mark Latham.

Sincerely,

Mrs. Nancy Singh

March 21, 2009

NANCY SINGH (MRS)
PO Box 5067
South Murwillimbah
New South Wales 2484
Import and Export Services

Mr. Harry Jenkins
Speaker
House of Representative
Canberra
ACT

Dear Mr Jenkins,

I watched the debate over the alcopops tax on Thursday, and Fair Work Australia on Friday. I have never felt so ashamed of so-called politicians, baying and snarling like wolves.

Part of the blame for the antics I witnessed would seem to lie with yourself. Why do you allow ministers to insult members of the opposition almost continually? Is it really parliamentary for Mr. Rudd to refer constantly to Mr. Turnbull as 'the Member for Goldman Sachs'? I thought he was the Member for Wentworth. Is it really proper for Miss Roxon to accuse the opposition of taking 'hush money'? I am baffled as to why you tolerate such bad behaviour and lack of respect. You do, by contrast, shout down those asking questions at every opportunity, calling your impartiality into question in my eyes.

The whole thing reminds me of the Jabba the Hutt scene in the *Return of the Jedi.* Not very nice!

Warm regards,

Sincerely,

Mrs. Nancy Singh

Speaker of the House of Representatives **Harry Jenkins MP**

Mrs Nancy Singh
PO Box 2067
NSW 2484

14 OCT 2009

Dear Mrs Singh

Thank you for your recent letter regarding the conduct of question time.

One of my concerns is that the rules applying to questions are much more prescriptive than those applying to answers and this can give the impression that Ministers have more freedom in what they say in their answers than those asking questions. The standing orders contain detailed restrictions on the form of questions, for example, they provide that questions must not contain arguments, inferences, imputations, insults, ironical expressions or hypothetical matter. As I have commented to the House in the past, a strict application of the standing orders would result in my ruling a large number of questions out of order. In the interest of sustaining a vital democracy, I apply the provisions relating to questions with discretion.

The rules of the House allow Ministers great scope in their answers. In answering questions Ministers may well refer to related matters which, even though technically they are in one way or another relevant to the terms of the question, do not satisfy the questioner, or indeed the television viewer. I assure you that I administer the standing orders as fairly and as effectively as I can. When Ministers attempt to stretch the rules too far I do rule answers to be not relevant to the question and I have sat Ministers down for that reason.

I attach a copy of an Infosheet on questions which you may find of interest.

Thank you for your interest in the work of the House.

Yours sincerely

HARRY JENKINS
Speaker

Parliament House Canberra ACT 2600 • Telephone (02) 6277 4000 • Facsimile (02) 6277 2050

March 21, 2009

Miss Jenny Macklin MP
Minister for Families, Housing, Community Services and Indigenous Affairs

NANCY SINGH (MRS)
PO Box 5067
South Murwillimbah
New South Wales 2484
Import and Export Services

Dear Miss Macklin,

I know it must be hard for you, being forcd to take responsibility for such a boring and thankless task as worrying about welfare claimants and dysfunctional Aborigine 'communities'. But I do think you should at least try to appear enthusiastic. Your replies during Question Time are as dull as dishwater.

Mr. Singh and I are winding down a few of our businesses to avoid the effects of the new Fair Work Australia unfair dismissal rules. So we have some money to invest, and thought we might lend to the Rudd Bank at 8%. Please would you send me the details of Mr. Rudd's account. I am enclosing $5 to cover postage.

It is good to see you make an effort with your hair and make-up and clothes, unlike Nicola Roxon who looks like she has slept in the bush for a week. Perhaps you could give her some tips on how to look good in clothes bought from op shops. She also needs to do something with her hair.

All good wishes,

Sincerely,

Mrs. Nancy Singh

PO Box 7576 Canberra Business Centre
ACT 2610
Telephone 1300 653 227
TTY 1800 260 402
Facsimile (02) 6244 7983
www.fahcsia.gov.au

MC09-009861

Mrs Nancy Singh
PO Box 5067
SOUTH MURWILLUMBAH NSW 2484

Dear Mrs Singh

Thank you for your letter of 21 March 2009 to the Minister for Families Housing, Community Services and Indigenous Affairs, the Hon Jenny Macklin MP. The Minister has asked me to reply to you on her behalf.

I note your comment that you enclosed $5 with your letter, however, when the letter was opened, no money was found. This apparent oversight on your part is fortuitous as Australia Post prohibits the carrying of currency notes or coins in its normal services.

For this reason, while your gesture is appreciated, I would be grateful if in future you did not send cash through the post.

Yours sincerely

Amanda Conroy
Ministerial and Parliamentary Services

29 April 2009

March 21, 2009

NANCY SINGH (MRS)
PO Box 5067
South Murwillimbah
New South Wales 2484
Import and Export Services

Miss Nicola Roxon MP
Minister for Health

Dear Miss Roxon,

I am writing to commiserate with you over your humiliating defeat in the alcopop wars. You should really have listened to my advice, as this was always going to end badly. I assure you that I am not one of those Gold Coast ladies who now refer to you as 'Nanny Rocks-off'.

I also think you should try to control yourself in the House. During Thursday's debate you came across as hate-filled, shrill and almost hysterical. Bawling like a fishwife is not a good example for young teenage girls.

Kind regards.

Sincerely,

Mrs. Nancy Singh

March 21, 2009

Mr. Wayne Swan
Treasurer

NANCY SINGH (MRS)
PO Box 5067
South Murwillimbah
New South Wales 2484
Import and Export Services

Dear Mr. Swan,

It is hard to believe it is only 9 months or so since I last wrote to you. At that time the economy was still purring along nicely, difficult though this is to credit!

There was some foolish panic over so-called inflation that turned out just to be price variations caused by the drought and oil prices. Mr. Glenn Stevens' handling of monetary policiy, I am sure you will agree, has been a shambles. He in effect triggered the slow-down as far back as June 2008, well before the collapse of Lehman Brothers. If I were in your shoes, I would call for him to fall on his sword.

It is a pity, too, that Mr. Rudd opted to spread gloom and doom, fear and trepidation, thud and blunder, instead of calmly reassuring people that the matter was manegeable and that the markets would recover this year. Mr. Obama has also done his best to make things worse. The prospect of out-of-control government spending is very worrying, all that debt for years to come.

NANCY SINGH (MRS)
PO Box 5067
South Murwillimbah
New South Wales 2484
Import and Export Services

Mr. Singh tells me that this is what left-wing governments always do, and that Mr. Obama and Mr. Rudd are using the recession as an excuse to spend like drunken sailors. He says Mr. Rudd is being reckless with our money. I find it hard to disagree, but I have pointed out that you are a strong and sensible man and would make a better Prime Minister that Mr. Rudd. None of the appallingly bad errors of economic management of the past several months are down to you, I am sure.

I am still backing you.

Sincerely,

Mrs. Nancy Singh

March 21, 2009

Miss Penny Wong
Senator

NANCY SINGH (MRS)
PO Box 5067
South Murwillimbah
New South Wales 2484
Import and Export Services

Dear Miss Wong,

I am not one to say 'I told you so', but I did warn you that your Green Paper idea was confused and unworkable. It must be humiliating for you, I know, that everyone can see what a mess has been made of things. But, as the poet says, 'you can't win with a losing hand'. I'd have a firm word with Mr. Rudd about his leadership skills if I were you.

Ever wishing to be helpful, I suggest you abandon the ETS forthwith and opt instead for a Carbon Tax. This would be much the same as the GST. Indeed, you could simply rename the GST the 'Green Security Tithe' and increase it to 20%. It would be easy to collect, would tax energy consumption in all its forms and would be transparent. Everyone who worries about global warming – I myself think it is based on deeply flawed ersatz science – could then congratulate themselves that they are saving the planet every time they buy something.

I am surprised you have not thought of this yourself before now. If you can think of arguments against such a simple yet effective measure, I should be glad to hear them.

Warm regards,

Sincerely,

Mrs. Nancy Singh

April 4, 2009

Mr. Kevin Rudd
Prime Minister

NANCY SINGH (MRS)
PO Box 5067
South Murwillimbah
New South Wales 2484
Import and Export Services

Dear Mr. Rudd,

As a former air hostess myself, I find it surprising that you should bully a young woman into tears. I know that it is upsetting if you do not receive the special lettuce you ordered – why are vegetarians such pains? But as you yourself said, mistakes happen and people are only human. You apology to this poor girl seemed very grudging.

I am sure you would agree that manners and proper comportment are important at all times, even when dealing with underlings and the common people. I find it hard to believe that you used the words 'useless fat slag' and 'incompetent slut' as reported. I am afraid you are getting a reputation for being rude and unpleasant.

But it is never too late to change your ways. As Edmund Burke himself noted:

> *Taste and elegance, though they are reckoned only among the smaller and secondary morals, yet are of no mean importance in the [conduct] of life.*

Sincerely,

Mrs. Nancy Singh

April 7, 2009

Prof. Glyn Davis
Chancellor
Melbourne University

NANCY SINGH (MRS)
PO Box 5067
South Murwillimbah
New South Wales 2484
Import and Export Services

Dear Prof. Davis,

It is a pity that your modest little 2020 Summit of barely a year ago has sunk without trace. Not much of a return for all those millions of dollars.

No matter, I was struck by your willingness to do business and your close relationship with the ALP. This is a great advantage, as I am sure you will agree.

One of my sons is not especially intelligent, but he has his heart set on being a Doctor. His father agrees that this would be better than allowing him to work in the family business. So we would like to buy him the necessary qualifications at your fine establishment. Please would you advise me on the best way to do this.

I am enclosing $5 to open our account in the meantime.

Sincerely,

Mrs. Nancy Singh

Glyn Davis AC
Professor
Vice-Chancellor

15 April, 2009

Mrs Nancy Singh
PO Box 5067
South Murwillumbah, NSW 2484

Dear Mrs Singh,

Many thanks for your letter to Professor Glyn Davis. The Vice-Chancellor was pleased to receive your kind words and has asked our Admissions Office to assist your family with an information pack outlining our available medical courses and their prerequisites for entry.

I am returning your $5 with thanks. Fees are only payable to the University following successful admission – full information on both full-fee and Commonwealth-supported places will be forthcoming, but I will advise that both forms of admission are entirely contingent upon academic achievement and merit. In your son's case, his eligibility for entry will most likely be derived from his HSC score, or any subsequent tertiary studies undertaken.

Yours sincerely,

Mike Flattley
Information Officer

cc. Ms Carmel Murphy, Deputy Principal (National Markets & Global Scholars), Office of Admissions

90371, 90367

Office of the Vice-Chancellor
The University of Melbourne Victoria 3010 Australia
T: +61 3 8344 6134 **F:** +61 3 9341 6060 **E:** vc@unimelb.edu.au

April 7, 2009

Mr. Craig Emerson MP
Minister for Small Business

NANCY SINGH (MRS)
PO Box 5067
South Murwillimbah
New South Wales 2484
Import and Export Services

Dear Mr. Emerson,

It is hard to believe that it has taken only 18 months for your government to preside over a recession, just as was the case under Messrs Whitlam, Hawke and Keating.

You are about the only government minister who understands the need to support small businesses through these turbulent times. This is the only way to save jobs in the short term until things get better, as they will. Giving out money in used $5 notes is perhaps not the best thing, but never mind. It seems to be very popular with the common people.

Mr. Singh sees an opportunity for a new line of business to complement our stable of family-owned enterprises. He thinks there is room in the market for more licensed brothels in northern New South Wales and South East Queensland.

He has asked me to write to you asking for details of government grants to set up business in the personal service sector. Please would you send me any application forms. I am enclosing $5 to cover postage.

I look forward to hearing from you.

Sincerely,

Mrs. Nancy Singh

April 7, 2009

Mr Joel Fitzgibbon
Minister for Defence

NANCY SINGH (MRS)
PO Box 5067
South Murwillimbah
New South Wales 2484
Import and Export Services

Dear Mr. Fitzgibbon,

I am sorry to see you have become embroiled in an *affaire du couer* involving Chinese spies and matters of High State. This reminds me a great deal of dear old John Profumo and the tart Christine Keeler.

As an Asian beauty myself, I understand the allure of oriental women to white men. We are so much more feminine and understand the ying and yang of sexuality and love. Australian woman are too angry and aggressive and driven by jealousy it seems to me.

It is perfectly reasonable for you to be drawn to the Jade Garden, but not to take a Chinese woman as a *paramour*. Madame Lui is not especially attractive really. You could do much better.

I should be grateful if you would send me a photo of your good self with Madame Lui, and am enclosing $5 to cover the postage. Many thanks.

John Profumo, of course, did the decent thing by resigning. I wish you well in your future career now that politics is a closed book.

Sincerely,

Mrs. Nancy Singh

April 7, 2009

NANCY SINGH (MRS)
PO Box 5067
South Murwillimbah
New South Wales 2484
Import and Export Services

Miss Christine Milne
Senator

Dear Senator Milne,

I know you must be very busy, but I am writing to you on behalf of the recently associated Currumbin Ladies Magic Circle. We should like to invite you to be our special guest speaker at our inaugural AGM and fundraiser in July this year.

We were hoping you might like to discuss the concept of Gaia, women's bodies, seasons and cycles and menstruation, *blood and the soil.* I personally find it helpful to think of Mother Earth rather than male science and sodomy. It is mud that binds the stones together.

The event will take place over a weekend, the date to be agreed once you have confirmed you can attend. You are welcome to stay longer and join us in meditation, a séance and other fun activities. I assure you there will be no frantic dancing naked nor kissing the whiskery chins of bogie men! There will be no men there at all.

I look forward to hearing from you. Please would you send me a picture of your good self and a short paragraph on your interests in politics. I am enclosing $5 to cover postage costs.

Sincerely,

Mrs. Nancy Singh

00.54

3004 0009371
POSTAGE PAID AUSTRALIA

The Tarkine
NORTH WEST TASMANIA

Thank you for taking the time to write to me. I would like to be able to respond personally to all the letters and emails that arrive in my office, but it simply isn't possible. My staff do, however, keep me well briefed on your letters and the issues that concern you. I also spend a lot of time out and about in the community, listening and responding to my Tasmanian constituents who are never short of good advice for their local Greens' Senator.

In Canberra, I am working alongside my four Greens' Senate colleagues to deliver better social, environmental and long-term economic outcomes for Australia. My portfolio responsibilities include education, climate change, energy, transport, biodiversity, biosecurity, corporate ethics, the new economy and small business, and World Heritage. Through my Senate committee roles, I am also helping to bring about positive changes for rural and regional communities, for consumers and in health care.

For more information on these portfolio areas and the work of your Greens' Senators, go to **www.christinemilne.org.au** and **http://greens.org.au**

You can also join the discussion on a fairer, more sustainable future at **http://greensblog.org**

HOBART MC 30AP

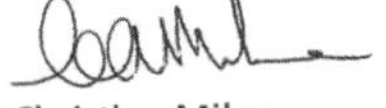

Christine Milne
Australian Greens' Senator for Tasmania
Spokesperson on Climate Change

THANK YOU FOR YOUR
KIND INVITATION.
SENATOR MILNE IS
UNAVAILABLE DURING
JULY FOR ENGAGEMENTS.

GPO Box 896, Hobart TAS 7001
PH 03 6224 8899 • FX 03 6224 7599
PHOTOGRAPH BY ROB BLAKERS

Authorised by Christine Milne, Parliament House Canberra • Printed by the Print Centre, 12-16 Bathurst St. Hobart

MRS NANCY SINGH
PO BOX 5067
SOUTH MURWILLUMBAH NSW

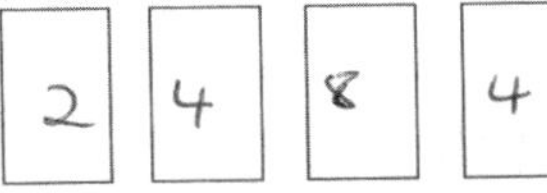
2 4 8 4

PRINTED ON 100% RECYCLED PAPER

April 8, 2009

Letter to the Editor
Mr. Robert Manne, *The Monthly*

NANCY SINGH (MRS)
PO Box 5067
South Murwillimbah
New South Wales 2484
Import and Export Services

Dear Mr. Manne,

I am writing to congratulate you on your brave decision to print Mr. Rudd's essay on neo-liberalism. It is a bit weak but at least the attack on capitalism has at last been rejoined. It is clear that this is the most serious post-war depression, and that all the nonsense about capitalism achieving permanent prosperity is just that – nonsense. It is good to see those who favour increased public expenditures winning the argument at long last. What we are seeing is a classic capitalist depression caused by greed and under-investment in infrastructure. This is simply the logical outcome to the fetishism of private capital as an ideology.

There is a positive side to all of this, as you will no doubt agree. Whenever major economic crises occur – $600 trillion in toxic debt! – practical politics take on a new urgency. The Left can now use the crises to further a hard-hitting political-economic program, and it is good to see President Obama doing exactly this The planks of this program, I submit, are as follows:

1. Raising unemployment benefits to the same level as the minimum wage, to be financed by a capital levy on all those with aggregates of capital over a million dollars, inheritance and capital gains taxation; at the same time removing the low paid from all income tax.

2. Nationalising key industries, such as telecommunications, the car industry, Qantas and hospitality and retailing;

3. A large-scale public works program to build schools and hospitals and universities, and inclusive cultural buildings; as well as a major investment in rail transport, road pricing and increased taxes on airlines;

4. Limiting all profits to 6% on invested capital, any surplus to be taxed at 100%

5. A 50% increase in public sector employment and pay to meet essential needs.

6. A ban on the ownership of second homes.

In this way, the crisis is an opportunity to demonstrate that only by resolute class-based political action can even the most elementary of economic demands and human rights be satisfied.

Sincerely,

Mrs. Nancy Singh

April 19, 2009

NANCY SINGH (MRS)
PO Box 5067
South Murwillimbah
New South Wales 2484
Import and Export Services

Mr. Barry Humphries
Presenter
Insiders
ABC Television
Melbourne

Dear Mr. Humphries,

Mr. Singh and I watch your programme almost every week. However, we are beginning to be dismayed by the lack of balance in your discussions with strong bias towards the radical Left. The discussion of the asylum seekers was very one-sided, or at least 3 to 1. We had thought you were supposed to be objective, but you regularly support the Left view, as it seems does everyone at the ABC. Please would you pass this observation on to the ABC Board.

I also distinctly heard the overweight woman panelist say 'Malcolm Turnbull is a piece of crap'. I am astonished that the ABC allows this sort of personal attack against a decent man.

She also said, and this is scarcely creditable, that it is the Opposition's fault that there has been an upsurge in boat arrivals – or perhaps it was David the Marxist who said this. Can you not find normal decent people with sensible views?

No doubt you shall all be supporting Mr. Rudd and the ALP during the next general election, just as you did in 2007. This is not how I expect my tax dollars to be spent.

Sincerely,

Mrs. Nancy Singh

June 10, 2009

Miss Yvette D'Ath MP

NANCY SINGH (MRS)
PO Box 5067
South Murwillimbah
New South Wales 2484
Import and Export Services

Dear Miss D'Ath,

I am not in the least surprised that you were unable to remember the size of the government's debt, as Mr. Rudd and Mr. Swan did their best to cover up the shocking amount of $300,000,000,000 plus interest. I don't know what they are thinking.

On the plus side, it was a pleasure to see your lovely smiling face in close-up. Mr Singh and I have followed your career as a backdrop for Mr. Rudd in parliament with much interest. You look much better when you smile. It is such a pretty smile. Might I suggest a little more highlighter on the cheeckbones and just a touch more eye shadow – just to give a little lift.

In fact, I was wondering if you would send a signed photograph of yourself for Mr. Singh as it will soon be his birthday and I know he would be thrilled. I am enclosing $5 to cover postage.

I look forward to hearing from you.

Sincerely,

Mrs. Nancy Singh

June 10, 2009

NANCY SINGH (MRS)
PO Box 5067
South Murwillimbah
New South Wales 2484
Import and Export Services

Mr. Bob Debus MP
Minister for Immigration

Dear Mr. Debus,

I am writing to wish you well in your retirement. I think you have made a wise decision, as you were clearly uncomfotable having to spin Mr. Rudd's line on the 'setting boats on fire incident' a few weeks back. It must be difficlt being plucked from obscurity for this thankless task.

It is clear that the government is losing control of illegal immigration and the boat trafficking.

I am hoping you will send me a signed photograph of your good self. I am enclosing $5 to cover postage.

I look forward to hearing from you.

Sincerely,

Mrs. Nancy Singh

June 10, 2009

Mr. Peter Garrett MP
Minister for the Environment

NANCY SINGH (MRS)
PO Box 5067
South Murwillimbah
New South Wales 2484
Import and Export Services

Dear Mr. Garrett,

I am writing to congratulate you on ending the government 'rebate' for so-called solar panels. I agree with you that this is just another form of 'middle class welfare', similar to the private health rebate, and is a waste of taxpayers' money.

All this whining about climate change is, as I am sure you agree, so much hot hair and PC nonsense. It is good to see you at last standing up to the climate change believers, most of them Leftists in any case.

Keep up the good work.

Sincerely,

Mrs. Nancy Singh

June 10, 2009

NANCY SINGH (MRS)
PO Box 5067
South Murwillimbah
New South Wales 2484
Import and Export Services

Mr. Harry Jenkins
Speaker
House of Representative
Canberra
ACT

Dear Mr Jenkins,

I am sorry that you have been so busy as to have been unable to reply to my last letter.

I am writing to say that I hope the new session of Parliament will be less demeaning than the last! The events of 28th May were truly shocking and, sad to say, made you look silly. I can still see Mr. Joe Hockey cutting up his chart into the approved size. It was very funny, but this is not the way we expect our representatives to carry on.

I think the probem lies with your leniency towards the Prime Minister, Mr. Rudd, and his frequent use of slurs, smears and nasty asides. I suppose this is why it is called 'Nasty Socialism'?

I do hope yiou can have a word with Mr. Rudd and stop this 'side show', as you quite rightly described it.

Warm regards,

Sincerely,

Mrs. Nancy Singh

June 10, 2009

Viewer Complaints
ABC Television
Melbourne

NANCY SINGH (MRS)
PO Box 5067
South Murwillimbah
New South Wales 2484
Import and Export Services

Dear Sir or Madam,

I wrote to *Insiders* on 19th April 2009, asking for confirmation of swearing and gratuitous insults on the programme. I distinctly heard the overweight woman panelist – Fran Kelly? – say 'Malcolm Turnbull is a piece of crap'. I am astonished that the ABC allows this sort of personal attack against a decent man.

Please would you advise me whether this bad language was indeed used (on a Sunday morning!) and what the ABC intends to do about it.

Sincerely,

Mrs. Nancy Singh

January 11, 2010

NANCY SINGH (MRS)
PO Box 5067
South Murwillimbah
New South Wales 2484
Import and Export Services

Mr. Tony Abbott
Leader of the Liberal Party

Dear Mr. Abbott,

I am writing to congratulate you on being elected Leader of the Liberal Party. I am also pleased to see you are not taken in by the Global Warming carpetbaggers. It was funny to see Mr. Rudd's face at the Copenhagen debacle, like a little boy who has had his toys taken away!

It is good to see a man with strong family values in a position of power. I was wondering if you would send me a photo of your good self. I am enclosing $5 to cover postage. Many thanks.

My prayers are with you in these interesting times.

Sincerely,

Mrs. Nancy Singh

January 11, 2010

NANCY SINGH (MRS)
PO Box 5067
South Murwillimbah
New South Wales 2484
Import and Export Services

Mr. Mark Thompson
Director General
BBC

Dear Mr. Thompson,

I am writing to say how much I enjoyed your interview with P.D James. It is no longer on the BBC web site of course, but happily can be found on You Tube. The old girl still has a razor sharp mind at 90, as is evident from the embarrassing stutters, evasions and unwilling admissions she drew from you. I think it was a pity that you started calling her Filly in an effort to curry favour. At one point your frustration was palpable, and I am sure I heard the words 'stupid old bat' muttered under breath?

I am not one of those who thinks the BBC is a bloated, politically correct, self-serving monolith that should be disbanded – at least I would not say so publicly. I retain a strong affection for the Beeb, even although the glory days of Blue Peter, Armchair Theatre, Monty Python, Life on Earth are long gone. Most of what you screen these days is puerile rubbish for the brainwashed masses, and propaganda for New Labour. I suppose you do what you feel you have to. Anyway, I am glad I don't have to pay the Licence Fee any longer. Australian TV is also rubbish, it is only fair to admit, and your cousin the ABC is just as bad for leftwing political bias and global warming ideology.

I was hoping you would be able to send me a photo of P.D. James and your good self. I am enclosing $5 to cover postage in these difficult and expensive times. My prayers are with you, and I hope you are able to save the BBC from its current course towards a sad demise and the failure of public broadcasting.

Sincerely,

Mrs. Nancy Singh

January 11, 2010

Miss Anna Bligh
Premier of Queensland

NANCY SINGH (MRS)
PO Box 5067
South Murwillimbah
New South Wales 2484
Import and Export Services

Dear Anna,

You may recall we exchanged correspondence a year or so ago, and you very kindly sent me a signed photo of your bonnie self.

I spent some time in Brisbane recently, a city that seems to be improving steadily and offers much better choice of eating establishments than it did only a few years ago.

However, one thing that dismayed me was the disgusting state of your taxi service. The cars are not clean inside and many of them smell of stale body odour. To my personal shame, it seems that this is the result of employing young men from India, most of whom do not wash. I was told a story – hopefully untrue – that on being forced to open the boot another young Indian was found asleep! This surely is not safe and is certainly unhygienic. The driver I had was a danger on the road, and didn't know where anywhere is! I cannot believe that you have personally authorized this?

The upshot is that I am now very reluctant to travel by taxi in Brisbane, and next time shall bring my own driver.

Keep up the good work.

Sincerely,

Mrs. Nancy Singh

January 11, 2010

NANCY SINGH (MRS)
PO Box 5067
South Murwillimbah
New South Wales 2484
Import and Export Services

Mr. Kevin Rudd
Prime Minister

Dear Mr. Rudd,

Welcome back to Australia from a freezing cold Copenhagen. Is it true that as well as making the weather hotter, climate change also causes cold weather?

Anyway, the good news is that you can dump the silly Emissions Trading Scheme, which no one understands anyway.

If I may say so, you did look a bit like a stunned mullet during the Copenhagen fiasco. I am sorry you have had such a rude awakening to the antics of the extreme left and the infantile greens.

Finally, I was wondering if you could send me the costs of the Australian delegation attending Copenhagen, both in dollars and carbon emissions. I am enclosing $5 to cover the costs of postage.

My prayers are with you in these difficult times.

Sincerely,

Mrs. Nancy Singh

January 11, 2010

NANCY SINGH (MRS)
PO Box 5067
South Murwillimbah
New South Wales 2484
Import and Export Services

Mr. Barack Obama
President of the United States

Dear Mr. Obama,

I am writing to congratulate you on a successful first year in office, including being awarded the Nobel Prize so soon. True, the recovery is still fragile and the level of government debt is a major worry, but I am sure you will sort this out in good time.

It is good to see a religious man with a young family at the helm. You are a very lucky man.

I was wondering if you would send me a photo of yourself, maybe with the family and your beautiful wife? I am enclosing $5 to cover postage. Many thanks.

My prayers are with you in these difficult times.

Sincerely,

Mrs. Nancy Singh

January 11, 2010

Miss Penny Wong
Senator for Global Warming

NANCY SINGH (MRS)
PO Box 5067
South Murwillimbah
New South Wales 2484
Import and Export Services

Dear Miss Wong,

You did look miserable in Copenhagen, poor thing. This is a shame as Copenhagen is a very fine city and the food is usually excellent. It was a bit cold, mind you, because of global warming. But the rent-a-crowd leftists must have come as a shock to you: all that venal hatred.

I would like you to comment on the leaked e-mails from East Anglia University, wherever that is, showing that senior pro-AGW 'scientists' have been falsifying the data and that there has in fact been a cooling since 1998?

Also, what is your opinion of the Mann 'hockey stick' chart, which we now know was faked. Was there a Medieval Warming Period? Was there a Little Ice Age? Were vines grown in North England in the 11th century? Has the earth never been hotter or colder than in the 20th century?

These events/phenomena point to a view that climate operates in long-wave cycles and that the current warming has little to do with carbon emissions from humans.

Still, I am afraid you and Mr. Rudd have made such a fuss about your ETS that you are stuck with it. My prayers are with you in these difficult times.

Sincerely,

Mrs. Nancy Singh

February 23, 2010

Mr. Peter Garrett
Minister for Roof Insulation

NANCY SINGH (MRS)
PO Box 5067
South Murwillimbah
New South Wales 2484
Import and Export Services

Dear Mr. Garrett,

I am writing to say how sorry I am you are getting the blame for the complete disaster that is the Government's Economic Security Strategy or GUESS, particularly in relation to pink bats. Australian wildlife never ceases to amaze me; I am sure there are very good reasons for throwing our hard-earned tax dollars about on these creatures, but for the life of me cannot think what these might be.

I suppose I must be a horrid little 'economic rationalist' but I don't believe people being electrocuted to death or houses bursting into flames is a price worth paying for a few mammals, pink or otherwise.

Whoever is responsible for this nonsense should be sacked. I am sure you will be able to find a culprit.

Please don't be tempted to go back to your day job! My prayers are with you in these difficult times.

Sincerely,

Mrs. Nancy Singh

Wakefield Press is an independent publishing and distribution company based in Adelaide, South Australia. We love good stories and publish beautiful books. To see our full range of titles, please visit our website at www.wakefieldpress.com.au.